THE HOUSE *on* SMITH LANE

A MAGNOLIA CREEK NOVEL

TERRI DEPUE

Copyright © 2021 by Terri Depue

ISBN   Softcover   978-1-953537-77-5

All rights reserved. No part of this book may be reproduced or transmitted in any form or by any means, electronic or mechanical, including photocopying, recording, or by any information storage and retrieval system without express written permission from the author, except in the case of brief quotations embodied in critical reviews and certain other non-commercial uses permitted by copyright law.

To order additional copies of this book, contact:
Bookwhip
1-855-339-3589
www.bookwhip.com

1

"All set," Tom said to Winnie as he walked back through the front door of Annie's house, rubbed his hands together to get them warm. "The car is running, and the heater is going full blast."

"Thank you so much for everything," Betty Lou said as Annie helped her and Lillian into their coats. "We do appreciate you including us old gals in your Christmas celebration."

Winnie, the third member of their little band of friends, was still talking animatedly to Annie's father, Pete who was helping her with her heavy coat.

"Oh, Annie it was such a wonderful day," Winnie said as she turned to hug the younger woman goodbye as she buttoned her coat. "I'm so happy for you and Tom!" Your grandma, Abby would be so pleased to see so much life in this old house," she added with a slight catch in her voice.

"We do miss her," Lillian added as she took her turn hugging her best friend's granddaughter. "But we love having you here, Annie."

"Goodbye, Pete. Goodbye Mary," Lillian called out to Annie's parents. "Enjoy the rest of your stay."

"Thank you, Lillian. It was nice to see you," replied Mary Reed with a wave as she stood beside her husband, Pete.

"Scott went out to start the car, and he said to tell you goodbye, Annie. I think the kids are already outside, but they're so wound up it's hard to keep track!" Becca admitted. "Thanks for everything, Becca," Annie said. "I don't know what I would have done without you this past year."

"Best friends forever, right? That's what we told each other when you moved away," Becca reminded her with a smile.

"That's right," Annie agreed, hugging her childhood friend.

"See you tomorrow," Susannah said to her nephew. "Just call me when you're ready, and I'll come by to pick you up. I'm looking forward to a couple of days having you all to myself!" she said excitedly, knowing that Tom and Annie would be looking forward to some alone time as well. They had a lot to celebrate!

"Okay, see you tomorrow," Ryan replied. He loved living with his dad, but he also missed his aunt. After all, she had been his mother after his mom died, and he'd lived with her practically all his life. He was looking forward to spending time with her as well.

"Goodbye, grandmother! Good-bye, grandfather. Merry Christmas!" Ryan called from the front porch, waving as Charlotte and Frederick Davidson headed toward their car in Annie's driveway.

"Merry Christmas to you too, Ryan," Frederick called out. "We'll see you soon. And don't forget to come to visit us. Maybe on your next school break? We miss you."

"You can count on it," Tom said, smiling as he stood beside his son, his hand on his shoulder. The darkness was settling in, and the shadows from the trees in the lane were long.

"Drive carefully, you two," Annie called from the door-way. "And thanks for making the trip to spend Christmas with us."

"It was our pleasure, and congratulations again on your engagement!" Charlotte added with a wave.

Arvin Sturgis stopped dead in his tracks at the sound of her voice. He quickly stepped back into the shadows of the trees that lined the lane separating his house and Annie's. Their voices carried across the wide of the front lawn and through the leafless winter trees as if they were standing ten feet away.

As the guests drove away in the opposite direction, the wind shifted and carried Arvin's scent across the yard. Daisy barked once, then started running toward the spot where Arvin stood. Or moved where he had been standing a moment before. As the couple drove off, Arvin quickly retreated up the road to his own house.

He could hear Ryan calls to the large golden retriever as he stepped around the side of his house and entered through the back door, the clean plate still in his hand. Arvin had been headed to Annie's house to return the plate and thank her for the meal she'd sent over earlier that evening.

His world had stopped when he heard the familiar sound of his wife's voice.

2

"I think that went well," Annie said to Tom as they finished cleaning up the dinner dishes. "I have to say I'm surprised Charlotte and Frederick stayed as long as they did after opening the gifts. Don't get me wrong," she said quickly. "I'm very happy they stayed. It just seemed like Charlotte was a bit uncomfortable here last night. Even Lillian noticed it. I half expected Charlotte to make an excuse to head home early today. Instead, they were the last to leave."

"Well, never underestimate the power of good food and a very happy grandson. Did he rake in the gifts this year or what?" Tom smiled, remembering the large number of presents under the tree for Ryan. "Then again, I don't know what has been normal for him."

Tom had known his son for less than a year. Ryan's mother, Maggie found out she was pregnant after they divorced and decided not to tell Tom at all. Fortunately for him, Maggie's parents and sister had not agreed with her decision to keep Ryan from his father. They located Tom after Maggie passed away last year. They felt it was important for him to have his father in his life. They realized their decision was a good one when they found Tom to be a good man and a stable influence on Ryan.

"Dad, can you come help me with the chairs?" Ryan called from the dining room.

"He told me this was his best Christmas ever," Mary whispered to her daughter as she brought in empty glasses from the living room.

"I have to say I agree with him on that one," Annie said as she looked at her engagement ring and smiled at her mother.

"I see you sent Ryan off with a plate of food and a Christmas pie for Arvin Sturgis. Has he been any friendlier lately?"

"No, I just thought it was a neighborly thing to do. I actually had Ryan invite him to join us for dinner since I know he's alone up there, but he declined. I figured a home-cooked meal and one of Betty Lou's pies might soften him up a bit. You just never know."

"Well I haven't seen him since I left for college, oh so many years ago," she said with exaggeration. "But he was several years older than me growing up so we didn't even ride the same school bus. I can't say I ever really knew him. I just knew of him. His mother died before I was born, and I remember your grandma, Abby telling me his dad died not long after we moved away. He was not a social person, but he would talk with your grandpa Ben about farming and the weather from time to time."

"Well then, maybe Arvin will eventually warm up to Tom. It would be nice to at least be on speaking terms with him."

"Speaking terms, with who?" Tom asked as he and Ryan came through the kitchen on their way to the basement with the extra folding chairs from dinner.

"Whom," Ryan corrected his father, smiling as he did so. "Okay, speaking terms with *whom*?" Tom said, turning to look at his son. He couldn't keep a straight face though, and they both started laughing as they continued down the basement steps without waiting for an answer from Annie, "Two peas in a pod!" Mary laughed, shaking her head as Annie watched them with amusement.

"Well, he's not wrong," Annie said proudly as she returned to drying the dishes.

3

Tom's upbringing groomed him to follow in his prestigious father's footsteps. The right schools the right friends, of course, the right girlfriends. His life in Magnolia Creek was far removed from that world, as was his fiancé. And that's just the way Tom wanted it.

His family was an important part of him. Their lifestyle was not. Tom had gone his own way, garnering his father's disapproval when he decided to quit law school to become an architect. His mother had eventually come around, financing Tom's schooling. Tom had long suspected that his father knew about the arrangement; it was unlike his mother to keep something like that from him, but he never mentioned it to Tom.

Harrison Walsh was a formidable man, equally comfortable making deals over cognac and cigars or on the back nine of the local country club. He was a man that made things happen. His family had been among the social elite in San Francisco for generations, and his marriage to his college sweetheart, Katherine Fitzgerald gained him entry into Boston high society as well. However, it was not only his position in the inner circle that kept him at the top of the list but also his reputation as a force to be reckoned with in the courtroom.

And that force would arrive in the small picturesque town of Magnolia Creek, Virginia, and tomorrow afternoon to have a serious conversation with his only son.

"Does he know?" Tom had asked his mother on the phone that morning.

"Yes, he knows. Please try to understand his position. It will make this much easier if the two of you can walk in each other's shoes for a time. Your father is a good man, Tom, and he only wants what's best for you. Unfortunately, he has a very different idea than you of what that looks like, Give him time. Help him to understand," she pleaded with her son. "I promise, I'll do my best to keep it cordial," Tom assured Kate before he hung up the phone.

"How about letting Ryan hang out with me for the day?" Annie offered as Tom sat at her kitchen table, contemplating how the meeting with his father would go. "That would give the two of you time to talk alone."

"That's a good idea, thank you. I'm trying to keep an open mind about this, but if you remember, I've had this discussion with him before. When I told him I was leaving law school. That did not go well."

Annie grinned as Tom's face contorted into an anguished expression at that memory. She stood up behind him and kissed the top of his head as he sat at the table, his head in his hands.

"You'll do great," she reassured him. "Just try to think about how you would feel if Ryan was dead set on doing something that you thought was a mistake."

"You are pretty smart, you know," Tom said to his bride-to-be thankful for her levelheaded advice.

"And promise me that you won't make this about me," she said as she poured him more sweet tea. "This is about your father and his expectations for your life. If you make it about me, I'm not sure you'll ever forgive him for trying to convince you to walk away."

"I'm not sure I can promise that," he told Annie, "but I'll do my best." "Okay, okay," Scott Jameson said as he came through the kitchen door. "You two save it for the honeymoon. Cover your eyes, Ryan," he called over his shoulder. "You don't need to see all this mushy stuff!"

Ryan slipped past Scott and turned to look at him long enough to roll his eyes. "They're just kissing, Uncle Scott. They do that all the time. I think it's kind of gross, but they seem to like it. Have you got any Gatorade, Annie?"

"Yes, and I'll get it for you while you go in the bathroom and wash up. Don't forget those elbows, Ryan inside and outside this time," she said loudly as he disappeared around the corner.

"What were you two doing, building a mud pit?" Annie asked, turning her attention to Scott.

"Nope," Scott replied. "We were washing your old truck. Remember to act surprised," he added with a wink, "when I found out that Ryan had never made a mud pie!"

Tom and Annie laughed as they watched their friend feign indignation. Over the past year, Scott had become Tom's closest friend, which worked out great for Annie. Considering Scott married her best friend from the third grade, it created that rare circumstance when couples both get along equally well.

"I told him that it was about time he learned, and I'm not sorry!" Scott said emphatically, sitting down quickly in Annie's recently vacated chair. "Just to be safe, you may want to go out the front door for the next few hours," he added with a sheepish grin. "I'm just saying."

"Honestly, I don't know which of you are worse," Annie told them. "You, and your mud pies or Tom, and his greasy bicycle chains. Between the two of you, I'm lucky he can even get clean enough to eat."

"Who needs to be clean to eat?" Scott asked, looking for Tom to Annie in mock confusion.

Ryan returned to the kitchen and proceeded to sit on the other side of his dad, wiping his clean but wet arms and hands-on his dirty jeans. Annie shook her head in disbelief. "Boys!" she said to no one in particular as she walked out of the kitchen, their laughter following her through the living room and onto the front porch.

Daisy had been lying on the back porch watching Scott and Ryan's mud bath, making no move to participate. She had followed them into the house and lay down on the rug in front of the sink. When Annie left the kitchen in search of a quiet place to make a phone call, Daisy followed. She lay down at the top of the porch steps, head resting on her front paws as she scanned the yard.

"I'm glad you're a girl," Annie said as she sat down beside her on the top step, scratching Daisy's head lightly. "And a clean one at that. Well, most of the time." She chuckled, recalling Daisy's encounter with the skunk last summer. That was wicked!

"Hello, my friend," Becca said when she answered Annie's call. "What's up?

"The boys have been playing in the mud," Annie told her childhood friend as she wrapped her sweater tighter around her against the winter cold. "I'm sitting on the front porch with the only other female in the house. How about dinner here tonight if you don't already have something planned? I can make spaghetti."

"Sounds perfect, Drew and I are in the grocery store now trying to decide what to make for dinner. I'll grab salad ingredients and fresh bread. Angela will be home from her friend's house at about 4:00 p.m. and we can come over then, if that's okay."

"That's great. You may want to bring clean clothes for your hubby, though. He was the one teaching Ryan how to make mud pies."

"Of course he was." Becca laughed. "Okay, we'll see you in about an hour."

4

"What you need is a diversion," Annie announced as she walked into Tom's kitchen early the next morning. "Your father won't be here until after lunch, so I put together a morning of fun and a picnic lunch."

"Ryan, why don't you go grabs your football and brings out the big water cooler from the garage? Just set it in the back of the truck, and we can fill it with water from the hose."

Ryan's eyes lit up at the suggestion of playing football, and he ran toward the garage without a word.

"It looks like I got here just in time," Annie said, noticing the cereal boxes and clean bowls on the table as she grabbed the milk carton and headed toward the refrigerator to put it back. "Breakfast is at the Jameson house, and then we all head to the park downtown. I'll grab a sweatshirt for Ryan whiles you…" Annie stopped as Tom reached out to her and pulled her close.

"It's all going to work out," she told him as she wrapped her arms around his waist. "You'll see. I have a good feeling about today. And not thinking about it for a few hours will help to ease the tension. After all," she teased him, "how can you be worried about meeting your father later when you're focused on not losing to a few girls now?

"Oh, so that's how it's going to be," Tom asked playfully. "Girls against boys? You don't stand a chance, you know."

"I wouldn't be too sure about that" she smiled. "Winnie has volunteered to referee!"

Laughing at the thought of Winnie with a whistle and grateful for the diversion, Tom quickly grabbed his gear and headed out to the truck with Annie. Ryan had already filled the cooler and was sitting in the back next to Daisy, casually tossing his football in the air.

They picked up Winnie on the way and were at Jameson's house in less than ten minutes. Becca was just pulling the second batch of biscuits out of the oven when they came through the back door.

"Right on time," she announced as she pushed the hot biscuits into a towel-lined basket that was already half full from the previous batch. "Take a seat anywhere." She nodded toward the big kitchen table. "Tom, can you please bring the pan of sausage gravy? There's a hot pad already on the table. Scott is getting the eggs, so we should be all set.

Okay, kids," she said in the direction of the family room, "it's time to eat!"

"Thank you," Tom said to his friends at the table, just loudly enough to be heard over the children's energetic chatter. "This is just what I needed." Annie squeezed his hand and Scott nodded knowingly. "It's our pleasure," Becca said, keeping her eyes on Tom as she reached for Drew. Her youngest was currently in the process of entertaining Ryan and grossing out his sister with half-chewed food that was slowly tumbling out of his mouth.

5

"Son."

"Father."

The two men shook hands as Harrison Walsh climbed out of the town car he had arranged to get him to Magnolia Creek. There was no airport in Magnolia Creek, so his company jet had landed at Richmond International. He had arrived in front of Tom's house moments earlier. As Tom approached the car, he could see through the windshield that his father was in the backseat on the phone. Tom waited patiently, knowing his father would finish his call before stepping out of the car.

"Bobby, how's the family?" Tom asked his father's driver when the other man exited the car.

"Sent the youngest off to college this year," Bobby told him, purposely leaving off the "Sir" when addressing the younger Mr. Walsh. It was at Tom's request and Bobby had eventually agreed. After all, it was he who had taught a young Tom Walsh everything he knew about cars and driving.

"It's been a while," Tom said as they shook hands. "You look good." "It's easy when you have a job like mine," Bobby said. "I get to drive fancy cars, read as much as I like and listen to my own music. Sure is better than a stressful corporate job!" he winked conspiratorially at Tom as he said this, knowing his employer's stressful corporate job was what paid his salary.

Bobby reached for the door handle just as Harrison Walsh put down his phone.

"You're looking well," Harrison said as he shook his son's hand. "It seems that this country air agrees with you," he added as they stood beside the car, the back door open as it idled quietly.

"Come inside where we can be comfortable," Tom said, gesturing to the front porch and the comfortable living room beyond.

His father didn't make any effort to move from his spot near the rear door of the car. "I thought we might get a bite to eat first. I have a table reserved for us at Bookbinders. I thought we could have a nice lunch and have a chat on the way."

"Actually," Tom began before his father interrupted him.

"You'll want to change, of course," he said patiently. "You can't go there in those clothes."

"Oh, that won't be necessary," Tom said with a smile, aware that he was still wearing the jeans and sweatshirt he had worn to the park that morning.

"There's no need to drive all the way back to Richmond for a good meal. We'll pop into the Victorian Café right here in town. When we're done, we'll come back here for some homemade pie. Ryan and Annie will be here by then, so you can meet them too."

Before Harrison could object, Tom tossed him the keys to his Porsche. "You drive. It's not far and, it's a beautiful drive with the top down." He did his best to suppress a smile as he watched his father hesitate for a moment, deciding what to do.

Harrison spoke briefly with his driver before walking over to Tom's car. "Are you sure you wouldn't be more comfortable driving?" Harrison said as he peered at his son across the car, Tom had already pulled the small sports car out of the garage and put the top down. "It has been some time since I've driven a sports car and, I'm unfamiliar with the area."

"Not to worry," Tom assured his father. "It's not far. You'll probably just be getting the hang of it when we arrive. But if you're afraid of…" Tom began, giving his father a concerned look.

"I never said I was afraid," Tom's father interjected quickly. "I was trying to be polite."

"Then let's go have some fun!" Tom said with enthusiasm, hopping over the closed door into the passenger seat. Harrison slowly removed his suit jacket and hung it neatly over the back of the driver's seat. He opened the door properly and lowered himself in behind the wheel. He adjusted the mirrors and started the car.

Tom gave him a sidelong glanced and watched with amusement as his father loosened his tie and let out a sigh. Tom directed his father along the river road, taking a long way around to give him a sense of the town. He could see that Harrison was beginning to loosen up, now that he'd gotten reacquainted with driving. He'd been chauffeured for so many years. Tom wondered for a moment if he should have asked his father if he still had a valid driver's license.

As they came into town from the other end, Tom also saw Magnolia Creek from a fresh perspective. It was a very quaint town with a rich history and beautiful old brick buildings. He took his father past Blooms, Annie's flower shop downtown on the square, and around the park where they all had been playing football earlier that day.

When they arrived at the café a few moments later, Harrison handed his son the car keys and smiled. "It's been a long time since I've had that much fun in a car," he said appreciatively.

"I'm glad to hear it," Tom said, taking the keys from his father. "It's important to get pleasure from the simple things in life."

6

"Good to see you, Tom," Marie said, giving him a warm hug. "Who have we here?" she asked pleasantly, noticing Tom wasn't alone.

"Marie, this is my father, Harrison Walsh's father, Marie owns this café and is personally responsible for the wonderful food served here."

"It's a pleasure to meet you, Mr. Walsh." "Harrison, please."

"This way, gentlemen," Marie said, indicating that they should follow her.

Marie seated them at one of the best tables in the house. The room had once been the parlor and boasted a beautiful hand-carved mantle over the fireplace and large low windows that overlooked the sweeping verandah. Large holly bushes filled pots on the porch, and a beautiful bouquet of red tulips adorned their table.

There was a small plaque leaning against the flower vase at their table with the inscription "Courtesy of Blooms, by Annie Reed." If Harrison noticed it, he didn't let on.

"Tom!" Chad said enthusiastically as he approached their table with a basket of freshly baked yeast rolls and a pitcher of ice water.

"Chad, I'd like you to meet my father, Harrison Walsh." Chad placed the basket of rolls on the table, wiped his hand quickly on his apron, and shook Mr. Walsh's hand. "It's a pleasure to meet you," he said politely. "Tom is a really great guy. You must be very proud of him," he said sincerely.

"Thank you," Harrison said as he shook the boy's hand. "You have a firm grip, young man. That shows character."

Chad immediately looked at Tom, who smiled and winked at him. "It certainly does," Tom agreed with his father. "Chad is Marie's son and quite a computer whiz. He is destined for great things."

Chad beamed proudly as he filled their water glasses and headed back to the kitchen.

"Speaking of destined for great things," Harrison said, looking at Tom over the top of his menu.

"Have you decided what you'd like to eat?" Tom asked his father, ignoring the obvious lead-in to the conversation that was inevitable.

"May I recommend the special, gentlemen?" Marie offered as she approached their table.

Father and son took her advice, and Marie left them to talk.

"Son," Harrison began, "you know why I'm here. Your mother has kept me informed of the situation with Ryan and more recently, your engagement to Miss Reed."

Tom nodded, ignoring the comment about Ryan being in a situation, choosing to hear him out before responding. After all, the man had come from San Francisco and it wasn't to have lunch at the Victorian Café.

"I suppose I understand to some degree why you didn't tell me yourself, but I have to say I'm disappointed that you didn't."

"I see," said Tom, knowing that his father was not done talking. "Tom, you are my son and I want what's best for you. I've worked hard to provide for my family and to ensure you a bright and successful future. Why do you fight me on this? First, it was law school, and now this," he said, gesturing around him.

"I'm an architect, father, not a lawyer. I know you're disappointed that I didn't follow in your footsteps, but you must know by now that it wasn't the right path for me. You taught me how to be successful, and I am. I built a thriving firm in LA, and I'm doing very well financially. I am in a position to provide a good life for my family, just as you did."

"Not just as I did," his father countered, struggling to keep his voice down. "You say you're an architect yet you walked away from your business, from your life. Who does that?"

"I seriously doubt that I could ever make you understand," Tom told his father resignedly. "I want to. Believe me, I want to. I'd like nothing more than to have you be a part of my life and that of my son. However, it has been clear to me for a long time now that your definition of success and mine are very different." Tom's statement was made with an air of finality that made a Harrison pause before responding to his son.

7

"I wonder how it's going," Annie said to Becca, trying not to sound concerned. They had been sitting in Becca's kitchen for the past hour, waiting for Scott to tell them that the coast was clear to head over to Tom's house.

They knew that Tom planned to take his father to the café, but he wasn't convinced that Harrison would agree to go. Scott offered to drive by Tom's house on his way back from the hardware store. He would text Becca if Tom's car was gone.

Scott's text came in a few moments later.

"Ryan, it's time to go," Annie said as she stepped onto the back porch. "Gotta go!" Ryan called over his shoulder to Angela and Drew as he raced toward Annie.

"Go tell Aunt Becca, thank you and we'll see her later."

As Ryan stepped inside to say goodbye to Becca, Annie took a deep breath and let it out slowly. She smiled at Ryan as he came through the door, and they headed to the truck. "Does Grandpa Walsh know about me yet?" he asked Annie as she backed out of Jameson's driveway.

"He does," she answered simply. What else could she say? She had no idea how the conversation with Tom and his father was going if he even wanted to see Ryan or her for that matter. Tom was convinced that his father was coming here to persuade him to return to LA, to his old life.

8

Their meal arrived, and the two men sat back in their seats while the food was being served. Tom took his cue from his father, who began eating without responding.

"That was delicious," Harrison told Marie when she stopped by their table a short while later.

"I'm delighted that you enjoyed it, Mr. Walsh. I mean, Harrison," she corrected herself quickly. "We have fabulous homemade desserts. I hope you saved a little room," she said, smiling and winking in Tom's direction.

A little room was laughable, Tom thought based on the portion sizes of Marie's desserts.

"Thanks, Marie, but we're having dessert at home with Annie and Ryan. Betty Lou baked us something special this morning, and it's a surprise even to me."

"Well, you won't be disappointed," Marie assured Harrison Walsh. "Betty Lou is famous around here for her baked goods. If you have a little time to visit, I can bring by some coffee."

"That would be great, Marie," Tom said. "Thank you."

"Okay, two coffees coming up. She smiled at the men and motioned for Chad to bring them two coffees.

9

"That smells wonderful, Betty Lou! You've outdone yourself, as usual." "Now, Annie. It's just a pie," Betty Lou said, pleased with the young woman's reaction. "It's coconut cream, dear. I hope Tom's father likes coconut cream," she said, worried lines beginning to form on her forehead. "I'm starting to wonder if I should have stuck with something basic like a deep-dish apple pie, or maybe a blueberry buckle."

"It's perfect," Annie said as she put a reassuring arm around her friend. "Now stop worrying or you're going to make me worry."

"Well, I may not know Tom's father, but I know Tom. That man loves you, he loves his son, and he loves his life here. There is nothing his father can say to him to make him return to his old life. To hear him tell it, he was miserable then."

"I know," Annie said. "I do know that. I'm just worried about Tom. It can't be easy for him to live with being a disappointment in his father's eyes. Tom is a good man. He runs a successful business, is doing a fabulous job at being a father and he is so big hearted. I don't think for a minute he will ever go back to that life. I just wish his parents would support him in this one. Can't they see how happy he is? I know his mom saw it when she was here last year. She told Tom that she had talked to his father about it and that's why he had decided to come and see for himself."

"Well, that sounds hopeful," Betty Lou said encouragingly. "It does, doesn't it? But Tom said I shouldn't get my hopes up. His father is very stubborn. It's more likely he's coming here to find fault with Tom's choices."

10

"I didn't come here to criticize you, Tom," Harrison began when Chad moved away from their table. "I came to try to understand why you choose to live in a tiny backwater town in the middle of nowhere. The people who are changing the world are not doing it from small towns, son. You're settling for so much less than you deserve."

"It's hard not to take offense at that statement," Tom said slowly, trying to keep calm, "but I'll try because I know you have no experience with living anywhere except large cities."

"That's not entirely accurate," his father interjected. "Cambridge is not a city and, I lived there for many years."

"Objection noted," Tom said, a bit harsher than he intended. "The point is," he began again, "life is different here, but for me anyway, it's better. I prefer living in a town where people know me by my name, not by my profession. I like that it doesn't matter how big or small my house is or what kind of car I drive. Here it is they who refrain from judging me with my fancy sports car and an expensive watch.

"There's nothing wrong with having nice things," his father told him. "You should not be judged because you have ambition and a desire to live a better life."

"That's just it," Tom said, feeling like he may actually be breaking through. "There is nothing wrong with those things. What's wrong is we need to show everyone how much we have. What's wrong is we need to know what others have and judge ourselves as less successful if they have more than we do. It is actually quite an insane and exhausting way to live. And that's exactly where I found myself last year. Racing hard and fast and getting nowhere that mattered. Nowhere that mattered to me," he added earnestly, hoping that his father was hearing him this time.

"Then take a vacation son, not a—"

"That's exactly what I did," Tom continued. "I took a vacation. I stepped out of the race and took a good look at my surroundings. That's when I saw the truth. I wasn't just exhausted. I was unhappy. There was nothing for me in that life. It was wrong for me. That's what I need you to understand. It was wrong for me. I took stock of where I was spending my time, whom I spent it with, and what I was getting out of the effort I was putting in. Do you know what I found?" He asked his father.

"Security," his father answered confidently. "Pride in making your own way in the world. Working hard while you're young so you can make a future for yourself and your family so you can enjoy your retirement."

"I found greed, father. I found greed in myself and those around me, and I was ashamed."

His father looked at him for a moment, his expression impossible to read. Tom considered that he was either going to argue in favor of greed or, more likely, try to convince Tom that he was wrong. Tom truly hoped that one day his father would take a look at his own life through a new lens.

"So you came here?" was all he said.

"I did eventually, but not at that moment. At that moment, I was on vacation in Nepal. Things get pretty clear up there, I have to say," Tom said lightly, hoping to keep his father from retreating to the safety of his prepared arguments.

"I didn't run away and end up here. It's quite the opposite, in fact. I chose carefully where I wanted to go and when. I planned to spend two weeks in Nepal, skiing with friends. God had other ideas. I broke my leg the first day out. I stayed at the resort for the first week. Being immobile provided me ample opportunity to think. After a week, I had made several decisions and I was anxious to put them in play to see where those choices led me."

"So you went from a ski lodge in Nepal to a little country town in Virginia?"

"No," Tom assured his father, "I was planning my journey. The destination became clear only after I finally decided what I wanted for my life."

Harrison sipped his coffee, sat back in his chair, and opened his mouth as if to say something. Tom waited for him to speak before continuing, but he thought better of it and nodded to his son to continue. "When I returned home after that first week, I realized that it was time for a change. It all seemed so logical sitting on a mountain in Nepal, but it felt even more right once I got back home. I had a party planned at my place for after our return, and I used that as the opportunity to tell my friends that I was leaving."

Harrison watched his son closely, but didn't speak.

"The woman I was dating was the first to leave. When she realized I was serious, she walked away without a word. To tell you the truth, I was pretty much counting on that reaction. After all, I had taken her to Nepal skiing with me, and she spent the entire trip with the others, even encouraging me to head home early. My friends had similar reactions to hers and left shortly after my announcement."

"What about your business? How could you walk away from a successful career?" his father asked him. "I get what you're saying about the girl and I've also had friends that turned out to be hangers-on if you will, but your career? You stood up to me for the first time in your life to convince your mother and me that you were destined to be an architect, and yet you walk away from a successful firm in LA, one that you built from nothing. That is the part I just cannot reconcile."

"But that's just it," Tom said with satisfaction. I didn't walk away from my business."

"So how does that work exactly," his father said skeptically. "You're living in rural Virginia, and your company is in LA?"

"Yes, the company is there, but the work is anywhere I choose. I took the company nationally in January. I hired executives to run the company, and I choose the jobs I want to do personally while the rest of the staff handles the bread and butter of the business."

His father began to smile.

"Weren't you the one who taught me that the only way to grow a business and guarantee residual income is to hire the right people and let them do what they do best?"

"Indeed I am," Harrison Walsh replied, slowly nodding his head as he realized that his son had been listening to him all these years.

"Father, I put the education you provided me to work in a way that I thought would make you proud. I don't want the same life you have, but I do want to provide for my family and help others that didn't have the opportunities you provided me. You and Mom showed me how important both are—you with your successful business and Mom with her charity work. I'm not rash and I'm not afraid of hard work. I just want to be working toward something I believe in and I want to enjoy the journey in getting there." Tom paused for a moment to take a long drink from his coffee cup. He wanted to let his father think for a moment about what he'd just said.

"When we started this conversation, I told you that your definition of success and mine are very different. That's not entirely true. We both value success in our personal and professional lives and care deeply about giving back to our communities. I just hope you can understand that success doesn't always look the same for everyone. And finding the right person to share that journey with, one who understands the courage it takes to change your life, well, that's what makes life worth living."

"I have to say I'm encouraged to hear you've actually given this a lot of thoughts and didn't just walk away from everything you worked so hard for, just to settle for less."

"Oh, I'm not settling for less," Tom said with a broad smile. "Speaking of Annie and Ryan," Tom said, glancing quickly at his watch for the first time all evening, "we should get going. They're both very excited to meet you."

11

"They're here! They're here!" Ryan announced when he saw his dad's car pull in the driveway.

"Okay, Ryan, calm down. Let's see if your dad is smiling before you go running out there," she said to the empty living room. Ryan was already sprinting across the front porch, anxious to meet his grandfather.

Tom intercepted his son with a hug and a kiss on the head. "Give your grandfather a minute, okay? He has to talk to his driver."

The limo had been parked in front of Tom's house for the past two hours, Bobby waiting patiently for his employer before returning to Richmond. Annie had invited him to wait inside, but he had politely declined, thanking her for the offer. "I always come prepared," he had informed her, indicating a cooler thermos, and several books and CDs. "You must be Ryan," Harrison said, holding out his hand in greeting as the limo pulled away from the curb and headed toward Richmond.

"Grandpa Walsh!" Ryan exclaimed as he slipped under Harrison's outstretched hand and put his arms around the older man's waist. "I've waited a long time to meet you," Ryan said eagerly. "You took so long I thought I was going to die!"

"Well then, it's lucky I got here when I did. And you can call me Grandpa Harry How's that sound?"

"Sounds good to me," Ryan answered, beaming. He led his grandfather up the porch steps to where Annie was waiting.

"Annie, this is my father, Harrison Walsh," Tom said, giving her a quick smile. "Father, I'd like you to meet Annie Reed, my fiancé."

"It's a pleasure to meet you, Annie. I've heard so much about you from Tom and Kate. To be honest, I think she knew Tom was in love with you before he did," Harrison said, winking at his future daughter-in-law.

"How is Kate?" Annie asked Harrison as he stepped up onto the front porch.

"Terrific, now," he replied with a slight smile, "but you can ask her yourself when she arrives tomorrow."

"Oh, that's great news!" Annie said happily, "I look forward to showing her what we've done in the shop since she was here last. I'd better give Gina a call and have her hold the apricot tulips. They're your mother's favorites," she said to Tom over her shoulder as she grabbed her phone and headed into the kitchen to call the shop.

Betty Lou was setting the table for coffee and pie when the Walsh men came into the kitchen. Annie watched from the back porch as Tom introduced his father to Betty Lou. There were such similarities in their physical appearance there could be no doubt that the two men were related. She couldn't be happier to see a reconciliation between Tom and his father.

"Two dozen's are good," Annie said into the phone. "Put them in two separate vases with matching ribbons. Tom's mother is coming to town tomorrow. I'll pick up one in the morning when I'm at the shop, and we'll leave the other one in the cooler for Kate to take home. Thanks, Gina," she said to her assistant before hanging up the phone.

12

"I appreciate you taking me to meet your friends," Kate told Annie as they drove out to Magnolia Lane to meet the ladies.

"It's no problem at all. They're anxious to meet you too," Annie replied, referring to her grandmother's closest friends who had taken her under their collective wing when she'd first arrived at Magnolia Creek. Of the three of them - Lillian, Betty Lou, and Winnie - Lillian had been the closest to her grandma, Abby. They had grown up together, much like Annie and Becca, and had lived their entire lives in the same town and with the same friends. Abby's death was hard on all three of the women, but Annie knew Lillian felt the loss more deeply. Betty Lou and Winnie were both a year younger and had been in the class behind Lillian and Abby all through school. Although they'd all been friends for as long as they could remember, Abby and Lillian were the heart of the little group. "It's such a pleasure to meet you, Kate," Lillian said warmly to Tom's mother. "I do appreciate you coming by to see me, but I hope you didn't go out of your way. You must want to spend as with your son and grandson."

"And my future daughter-in-law," Kate added, turning to smile at Annie who was seated beside her in the sunroom at Magnolia Lane. "But I assure you it was no trouble. When Annie told me about your new home, I just had to see it for myself. It's a truly remarkable property."

Lillian took the opportunity to tell Tom's mother about the nursing home prior life at the local high school and how she and her friends and all their children had attended there before the new school was built a few years earlier.

"Lillian, this is so warm and inviting," Kate said when the older woman took them upstairs to see the room she shared with Eva Gordon. "Please have a seat," Lillian said as she motioned to the small conversation area under the windows. We have a few minutes before we have to leave, don't we, Annie?" She asked.

"Yes," Annie confirmed, checking the time. "I told Winnie and Betty Lou we would meet them at the café in about an hour." Just as they were getting settled, Eva returned and, Lillian introduced her to Kate.

"Your son is a true blessing to me," Eva said earnestly. "He's such a wonderful young man. I don't know what I would do without him. I really don't," she said, smiling at Kate as she took her seat.

"He thinks the world of you too," Kate assured her. "He is so happy to have such a lovely home to care for and, I can't tell you how much he enjoys the yard work and gardening. It is good for him to be out of the city and getting so much fresh air. I can see that he is happy."

They insisted that Eva join them for lunch at the café, where Kate learned more about all of the women and their families.

"What did you think?" Annie asked Kate as they drove home a short time later.

"It was such a pleasure to spend time with them all," Kate told her. "They certainly are charming southern ladies."

"They are," Annie agreed, "but I meant about the concept at Magnolia Lane?"

"Oh, Annie, it was remarkable!" Kate effused. "I can't wait to talk with Harrison about your idea to start a program across the country for repurposing these old majestic buildings. I can even see it expanding to include old courthouses, fire stations, or any old building with grand architecture and solid structure. It's brilliant!" she exclaimed, excited at the possibilities.

"I just knew you'd see the potential," Annie told her future mother-in-law happily. Annie had always loved the idea of reusing old items for new and unique purposes.

Why should beautiful buildings be any different? *I hope this catches on*, she thought excitedly. If anyone can make it happen, it's the Walsh family!

13

"How long can you stay?" Tom asked his father. They were walking around the den looking at pictures of some of the more impressive buildings Tom had designed.

"I fly out of Richmond on Monday," Harrison said with a touch of regret. "I have clients to prep for court on Tuesday. I hope you understand." "Of course," Tom said, understanding that his father was a busy man.

"If I had known things were going to turn out this way to Tom, I would have made arrangements to be away from the office longer," Harrison said sincerely.

"It's really no problem, Dad. It's not like we won't see you for a year," he said with a grin. "After all, you have a new grandson to spoil, and there is a wedding coming up this summer!"

Harrison Walsh reached out and hugged his son. Tom was startled but recovered quickly and hugged him back. The last hug he remembered from his father was during his grandfather's funeral, and it was in front of everyone, not a private moment like this.

"That's the first time you've called me Dad since you were a little boy," he said softly.

Annie and Kate watched the two men embrace and then looked at each other, unable to believe what they'd just seen. They stepped quietly from the doorway to the den and hugged each other excitedly.

"If I hadn't seen it with my own eyes," Kate began. "I wouldn't have believed it," Annie concluded.

"Wouldn't have believed what?" Ryan asked as he came in from the kitchen with a handful of cookies.

"Ryan Davidson Walsh!" Annie scolded him with mock seriousness. You know better than to jump into the middle of adult conversations." "Yes, ma'am," he said, surprised at Annie's reaction, a cookie halfway to his mouth.

"Go back into the kitchen, wash your hands, and get a plate of those cookies. When you're done, come right back in here and take a seat with your grandmother and me so we can tell you what's going on," she finished with a smile.

Ryan grinned, shoved the cookie in his mouth, and ran back into the kitchen to quickly wash up.

14

Grandpa Harry, Ryan, and Tom spent the afternoon planning the best indoor backyard barbeque Tom could arrange. He decided that he'd call in the "big guns" to impress his dad, so he asked Scott to come early and

Prepare his famous ribs. Marie offered to bring fried chicken from the café, and Lillian went to Betty Lou's house to help her bake pies. It would just not be a Magnolia Creek barbeque without Winnie's homemade macaroni and cheese, so Tom added that to his list as well.

Tom texted Annie the list of supplies they'd need, and she and Kate picked those up while Becca and the kids made decorations. After all, it was a party!

"I can see why you like it here, Tom. The people are so genuine," Kate told her son that afternoon. He had taken a short break from playing host and now sat in the chair next to her just inside Eva's garage, the fire pit a mere three feet outside the big doors. They sat there for a few moments in silence, enjoying the scene in front of them. Although the weather was mild, it was still January, and the fire pit Tom and Ryan built last fall was a popular gathering spot.

"I had the opportunity to talk with that nice young man earlier today," Kate said as she and Tom watched Chad play flashlight tag with the younger kids. "He doesn't make it too easy for them, but he always lets himself get tagged. He reminds me of you."

"Tom deserves the credit for that," Marie said as she took a seat opposite Tom and Kate, slightly closer to the warmth of the fire. "I don't know what I would have done or where Chad would be now if Annie and Tom had not intervened. Thankfully, they did, and I am so proud of the young man my son is becoming."

"He's a good kid, Marie, and you've done an amazing job raising him on your own. He just got in with a couple of kids who haven't had positive male role models in their lives," he explained to his mother, and he couldn't see a way out."

"Well, regardless of what he's done in the past, anyone can see his character now," Kate said sincerely. "He is respectful to his elders and kind to the younger kids. I'd say you have good reason to be proud of your son, Marie. I know I'm proud of mine," she added, smiling at Tom.

Harrison and Kate attended church with Tom, Annie, and Ryan the next morning where they met Pastor Bob, Who would be officiating at Tom and Annie's upcoming wedding. Ryan introduced Grandpa Harry to his friends on the baseball team and practically anyone else he could find. After the service, they joined Lillian, Betty Lou and Winnie at the Victoria Café for a pot roast lunch.

"Aunt Susannah used to work here," Ryan told his grandma as they were being seated. "She used to walk people to their tables and bring home fresh biscuits."

"Is that so?" Kate said thoughtfully, trying to remember what she'd been told about Ryan's aunt Susannah.

"She was my mom after my first mom died," he offered freely. By the time the water glasses are filled and the bread served, Ryan had filled her in on everything she needed to know about his aunt, Susannah.

15

The weekend had passed by too quickly, Annie thought as she headed over to Tom's house to say goodbye to Kate and Harrison.

"Thanks so much for taking me around to meet your friends and see your shop. You've truly made Blooms into an inspirational and inviting space," Kate told Annie as she hugged her goodbye. "It must have been magical over the holidays. I'm sorry we missed it."

"Me too," Annie replied. "For a lot of reasons," she added remembering their wonderful first Christmas in Magnolia Creek and Tom's memorable proposal.

"We won't miss the next one," Kate assured her. "Will we, Harry?" Kate asked her husband in a way that could never be construed as a question.

"Not a chance," Harrison assured his wife with a smile. "Sir," Bobby said as he came to the door, "whenever you're ready."

"Well, we have a plane to catch," Harrison joked, knowing full well that his company plane was not leaving without him.

"Thanks, Dad," Tom said to his father as he walked him to the waiting car. "I appreciate you taking the time to come out here to talk to me. It means a lot to me."

"To me too, son. I had the situation figured all wrong. That doesn't happen often," Harrison told his son without a hint of conceit.

"I love you, Tom. You know that right?" his mother asked him directly as she looked into his eyes.

"I've always known that, Mom," he replied with a smile. "Now go get in the car before Dad."

"Kate? We need to go," Harrison said, loudly already returning to business mode.

"Yells," they said in unison, sharing a laugh at Harrison's expense.

As Tom's parents drove away, Annie leaned into Tom and put her arm around him, only partly to keep warm.

16

"Happy birthday!" Pete and Mary said in unison when Ryan answered the phone.

"How was the party?" Pete continued before Ryan had a chance to greet them.

"Hi, grandma! Hi, grandpa! It was so cool! Dad drove us to Richmond to play paintball!"

"That sounds like the best party ever!" Pete said excitedly, attempting to match his new grandson's enthusiasm.

"Oh, and then we had pizza at that place where you can eat as much as you want. And we didn't even have to wash up and change our clothes first. We got to go with paint all over us!"

"That certainly sounds like a kid's dream birthday party," Mary interjected with a laugh. "Did you have a birthday cake at the pizza place too?"

"No, Annie made me an ice cream cake that looked like it had paintball splatters all over it. It was so cool! We got to eat it on the back porch with our hands," Ryan said, clearly still flying high from his best birthday party ever.

"We're glad you had such a fun day, Ryan. We wish we could have been there, but we'll come to visit soon. Tell your dad we said hello."

"Okay, bye!" Ryan said as he handed the phone to Annie and ran back outside to his friends.

"Well, he seemed excited," Mary said to her daughter with a laugh. "Whatever made you think of letting them eat ice cream with their hands?" "It just seemed like a messy day and with a bunch of energetic boys, messy just works," Annie replied. "It's also been really warm here for February so, I was able to send them outside to eat it. I have to admit, they are probably wearing almost as much of the cake as they ate. They had such a great time it was totally worth it. Besides, Tom can just hose off the back porch when they're done so cleanup will be a breeze!"

"You always were good with kids, honey. That's what made you such a great teacher."

"Thanks, Mom. I do miss it sometimes, being around the kids mostly, seeing their eyes light up when they learn something new. To be honest," Annie admitted, "the life I have here is more fulfilling. It's like a dream come true when I didn't even know I had the dream. Crazy, right?"

"Not at all," Mary said encouragingly. "Sometimes we start down a path in life that is a really good fit for us and we're happy. Then something different suddenly appears and if we are brave enough to take a chance, we find our true path. I believe that's what happened to you, Annie. Somehow, I think your grandma, Abby just knew you belonged in Magnolia Creek. God rest her soul."

"Well, she was right. This is home. But I miss you and Dad so much," Annie added sadly.

"We miss you, too, honey. More than you know. Okay, enough of that for now," Mary said, shaking off the melancholy. "Let's talk about your wedding! So, Becca and Scott will be your matron of honor and best man?" "Yes," Annie said enthusiastically into the phone. She was curled up on the sofa in the living room with a cup of hot tea and sixty pounds of warm love snoring at her feet while Tom wrangled a dozen hyper kids in the backyard.

"Ryan will be the ring bearer, and Scott and Becca's daughter, Angela will be the flower girl. She and Ryan are the same age, so it worked out perfectly.

"What about attendants? How many are you planning on having and have you decided who to ask?"

"We both really wanted to keep it small so, we decided we don't need additional groomsmen or bridesmaids. The ceremony will be held in the small chapel that was part of the original church. It will hold fifty people, and we are only inviting thirty so we'll have plenty of room."

"It sounds perfect, Annie. I remember going to church there when I was a little girl. In fact, your grandma Abby and grandpa Ben were married in that little chapel. It's going to be so beautiful, honey."

"I think so too. The ladies have been such a huge help to me already, and Betty Lou was able to talk with Pastor Bob and get the date we wanted." "Have you had a chance to think about the reception or the rehearsal dinner?"

"Actually, Tom is taking care of the arrangements for the reception. He and Ryan are planning to have it in the backyard at their house. That way it can be a surprise for me to see it for the first time after the wedding." "I'm sure they are having a good time working together on it to surprise you."

"They are. They love to pretend to be having secret conversations about something when I walk into the room. Then they make a big production out of shushing each other. It's actually quite comical."

"Oh, and we thought we would have the rehearsal dinner at the Victorian Café. Marie has already worked up some sketches of how she'd like to set it up. I can't wait for you to see them. She has a wonderful area in the side yard with winding paths and natural archways. It's a very romantic setting. The big trees are lit up in the evening, and it's almost magical out there. In fact, Tom and I went there for Valentine's Day this year."

"Wow, it sounds like you really have things under control."

"You would think so, right?" Annie laughed nervously. "The truth is, some days I think I have it all together, and other days I feel like I'm missing something huge. There are so many arrangements to make, and it feels like a house of cards. If even one piece doesn't go as planned, the whole thing could come crashing down."

"Well, as long as you and Tom and Ryan are there, that's all that truly matters. As far as the other pieces, maybe I can help. Your dad and

I have been talking," Mary told her daughter, "and we'd like to come for a visit this spring."

"Really? Oh, Mom, that would be great!"

"We thought we'd come out just before Easter and maybe stay two or three weeks. Dad feels that he can get away for two, but depending on how things are going, I may be able to stay a little longer."

"That would be perfect, Mom. I could really use your help to pull this all together. My friends have been absolutely fabulous, but you're my mom. I'd really love for you to be a part of this."

"Thanks, honey. We want to be there too. We're so far away now, and we really miss you. Phone calls are great, but it's not the same as being with you. Now hang on a sec. Your dad wants to talk to you for a minute."

"How's my girl?" Pete's voice came booming over the phone. "I'm great, Dad! It's so nice to hear your voice."

"I usually like to, just let you gals catch up, but I wanted to talk with you before you hang up. Now you know, I can't sit around doing anything all day so, I expect you to have some projects or something for me to work on while I'm there. I know Tom is as handy as they come, but I have to think there are some things that are just a two-man job. And he's a new dad so, he probably doesn't have as much time as I do to work on projects." "I'll tell him to start making a list" Annie replied, knowing her dad would definitely need something to do to keep busy. Although he ran the family plumbing business in Seattle, he was an all-around handyman and could make or fix just about anything.

"Okay, well, that's all I had to say. I'm sure your mom updated you on anything else that you need to know. We'll be in touch when we get the reservations made. We're really looking forward to seeing you, sweetheart. Your mom misses you a lot."

"I miss you too, Dad," Annie said softly, knowing exactly what her dad was saying.

As Annie hung up the phone, she started laying out in her mind what needed to happen over the next few months and specifically what needed to be taken care of prior to her parents' visit. She knew she would put her parents in her mother's old bedroom where they had stayed last

Christmas. However, with Ryan moving into the room at the end of the hall, she had moved several things into her parents' room that would need to get sorted out and stored somewhere else.

As she headed up the stairs with Daisy following close behind, she realized she was quite excited about the prospect of her parents coming for an extended stay. They had only been able to get away for a few days over Christmas so this was going to be a nice, long visit.

17

"Grandma and Grandpa Reed are coming to visit soon," Annie announced at dinner.

"Cool!" Ryan said happily. "Grandpa told me at Christmas that the next time he came for a visit; he would teach me how to whistle. How cool is that?" he exclaimed as he looked happily at his dad.

"That's very cool, son. Maybe he can teach me too," Tom said with a smile. "And that's great news for you too, Annie. I know how much you miss having them close. Did your mom say how long they'd be staying?"

"At least two weeks, maybe three. Dad thinks he can get away from his business for two weeks, but even if he has to go back, Mom may stay for another week to help me with wedding planning."

"That's great! I'm looking forward to spending time with them. I have a feeling I can learn a lot from your dad. We didn't have much time together over Christmas."

"It was a little hectic," she said, smiling as she remembered her first Christmas party at the house, filled with family and friends. And, of course, there was the proposal. Annie looked at her fiancé and his son, smiling as she remembered their first Christmas together.

Tom returned her smile instinctively, knowing what she was thinking about it.

"Speaking of learning from him, Dad made a special request that we have a list of projects for him to do while he's here. He's really happiest when he's busy and loves to work with his hands. Do you think we can come up with something for him to work on?"

"Leave it to me," Tom said confidently. He had several projects around Eva's house that Pete would be a huge help with, especially those involving plumbing. Lately, he'd been tossing around the idea of making something special for Annie, and he knew that would be a great project for him, Pete, and Ryan to work on together. Since he'd arrived in Magnolia Creek, Tom had been thinking of getting into furniture making. Not because he didn't have enough to do but because he had a real passion for it. It occurred to him that Pete and Mary's visit may be the perfect time to start. Now, all he had to do was figure out a way to keep Annie from finding out about the new large rocking chair he'd designed for her front porch.

18

The wedding dress was right where Annie had left it in the corner of the attic by the full-length mirror. As she made her way toward it, she felt close to her grandmother. "I just hope it fits," she said aloud, sure that grandma,

Abby was listening. She slowly removed the cover that had been protecting the dress for over half a century, hoping to keep the dust from clinging to the delicate fabric. It had been nearly a year since she first discovered the dress, the day she and Becca had gone exploring in the attic for the first time.

"Annie?" Tom called from the bottom of the stairs. "Are you up there?" "Yes, but don't come up here," she replied quickly.

"Okay," Tom replied hesitantly. "Ryan and I are heading over to Scott's to pick up his spreader. He's loaning it to me so I can get the fertilizer down this weekend."

"Okay, have fun!" she called back, clearly distracted by whatever it was she was doing up there.

"Are you sure you don't need my help with anything?" he said, putting his foot on the bottom step. "There's no need for you to be moving anything heavy." Although they were not yet married, he took pleasure in his role as man of the house.

"Nope, I'm good. Bye!"

"Okay, we'll be back shortly." *What was she doing up there?* He wondered. Before he could come up with a plausible explanation, his thoughts were interrupted by what caught his eye out the bedroom window that overlooked the backyard. Ryan was walking proudly toward the back porch with a large snake dangling from his right fist.

Tom headed quickly downstairs to intercept him before he attempted to bring the squirming reptile into Annie's house. "What do you have there?" he asked his son nonchalantly as they met at the bottom of the back porch steps. "Just a little old garter snake," Ryan said, trying to appear as if it was a common occurrence.

"Wow, I'm impressed. Those things are fast. How did you manage to catch it?"

"Well," Ryan began, beaming with pride, "it takes a combination of skill and planning."

'I can't wait to hear how you pulled that off," Tom said sincerely, "but first, I need to know what you plan to do with it."

"How about I keep it in my room?" he asked with wide eyes and a hopeful expression on his face.

"How about no?" Tom said firmly. "It would hate being in a cage when used to being free. Do you really think that's the best way to go?"

"No," Ryan answered honestly. "Besides, if I let it go, I can always catch it again," he said confidently, as he released the snake and watched it slither swiftly toward the high grass behind the barn.

"Good thinking, son. Now, hop up into the truck and tell me all about your impressive skills and planning on the way to Uncle Scott's house."

"Well, it's like this," Ryan began as he relayed his snake-catching tactics in detail.

Tom loved listening to his son. He could hardly believe that barely less than a year ago he had no idea he was a father. It was like having a wish come true that you never knew you had.

In that time, Tom had transitioned from an unfulfilled existence that, at least outwardly, most people dream about, to having everything he wanted in a life most people have but don't appreciate. Tom was truly grateful.

19

"So, Becca asked excitedly, "does it fit?"

"I haven't tried it on," Annie confessed as she and her childhood friend made their way to Annie's bedroom.

"I was hoping to be here when you did," Becca said with a hint of relief in her voice.

"It didn't seem right to try it on without you. After all, you were with me when I found it."

"So what are we waiting for? Let's do this!" Becca said enthusiastically, eyeing the dress hanging from the top of Annie's open closet door.

Annie slowly and delicately slipped the antique dress over her head while Becca tugged very gently to pull it down and smooth it out. The white silky fabric was in excellent shape for the age of the dress, but Annie was terrified of ripping it in a place that would not be easy to mend.

Unfortunately, the veil had not fared as well as the dress and was not usable. The dress would need a few minor repairs for some missing sequins, but those could easily be pulled from the remnants of the veil they had salvaged.

As Becca finished hooking the back of the dress, Annie's eyes began to fill with tears. It felt so right to be staring at herself in her grandma, Abby's wedding dress. Her mother's wedding dress had been ruined when their roof leaked into the attic. Annie was a young girl at the time, and her mother had cut down the dress and let her daughter use it for dress-up. Now, as she stood and looked at herself in the full-length mirror, she felt a strong sense of belonging belonging in this house and this life, marrying Tom, helping him to raise Ryan, and running a successful business. Annie had known, almost since her arrival, that her move to Magnolia Creek was the right one. She was living the life she never dreamed of yet always wanted.

She had to think that Grandma Abby somehow knew this was where she belonged. She could easily have left the house and property to her daughter Mary, yet she chose Annie.

"It's perfect, Annie," Becca said softly at Annie's reflection in the mirror as she looked over her friend's shoulder and hugged her gently.

Annie sobbed with one quick draw of breath as warm tears began to slowly roll down her face.

Becca, in her role as matron of honor and best friend, had come prepared. She pulled a tissue from her pocket and handed it to Annie.

"It's all working out just as it's supposed to, Annie. Tom is a wonderful man, and he loves you. You are where you're supposed to be. It's a little scary, isn't it?" she asked, smiling at her friend in the mirror.

"You could say that," Annie replied as if it were an understatement. "I think I just realized that I've been holding my breath for months." The realization of her words brought a smile of relief and with it a fresh round of tears. "Then I think it's high time you breathe, my friend. Turn around here and hug me."

"Thanks, Becca for everything. Who knew when we were eight years old that we would be standing here together twenty years later?"

"Actually, we did," Becca said as she remembered their childhood pact. "We sat in my backyard and promised that we would be friends forever." "And then we moved away," Annie said, her voice catching at the memory of how painful it was to leave her home. "Okay, that's enough of that," Becca said with mock seriousness as Annie regained her composure.

"You're here now, and we have work to do!"

Annie and Becca spent the next few hours talking about details of the wedding, looking through bride magazines, and laughing about childhood memories. Some of the biggest decisions had already been made, but there were plenty of smaller ones that needed to be finalized. They had multiple lists and were finally at a point where they were checking off more items than they were adding.

20

Annie had met her neighbor Arvin Sturgis only once, and it was not exactly a friendly conversation. She had been at the hardware store about a month after moving in when she heard the cashier thank him by name.

Annie took the opportunity to introduce herself. "I'm Annie Reed, your new neighbor."

"I know who you are," he said gruffly. "I, uh, heard your grandmother passed." He looked at her quickly with sadness in his eyes, nodded his head curtly, and turned to leave. "Well, I just wanted to introduce myself..." she began, her words trailing off as she watched him disappear through the door without a backward glance.

"Well, that was rude" Annie mused aloud as she walked to the counter with her purchases.

The tall, lanky young man behind the counter stood up from where he had been stocking small boxes of hardware and, shaking his dark hair out of his eyes, smiled with understanding.

"Oh, don't mind him," he told Annie. "I've lived here all my life and have never once seen that man smile. Sad, isn't it?" he asked, looking toward the front door where Arvin Sturgis had been a moment ago.

It certainly was, Annie had replied agreeably, still wondering about her neighbor and chiding herself for not being more gracious about his abrupt manner.

Annie had not given much thought to her reclusive neighbor, until today. She could hardly believe her eyes when she stepped quietly into the clearing by the big oak tree and found the older man sitting on the grass with his back to the tree staring at the swing gently moving in the breeze. In fact, it appeared that he was talking to someone on the swing. Was he hallucinating, she wondered, or just remembering? She couldn't be sure, but one thing was certain, she was intruding on the man's privacy. She turned slowly to go back the way she came, hoping to retreat unnoticed.

Daisy wasn't quite as considerate. The large dog spotted Annie from across the clearing where she had chased a rabbit down a hole. Daisy made her way toward Annie, barking continuously and tail wagging vigorously. Daisy did not have a stealth mode, Annie thought as she winced at the racket Daisy was making as she made her way across the clearing toward her owner.

Annie's heart sank, along with her plans of sneaking away unnoticed. She stole a glance in the direction of the tree to find Mr. Sturgis making a hasty departure in the opposite direction. As unintentional as it was, Annie knew that she had intruded on her neighbor's solitude. This spot held some significance for him. Annie had seen the tree swing on one previous occasion when she was out with Daisy, but it had not occurred to her that it might be on Mr. Sturgis's property.

21

"Do you know someone named Margaret?" Annie asked the ladies as they enjoyed the mild weather on the terrace at Magnolia Lane. "I came across the most beautiful old oak tree with a tree swing the other day," she told them. "The tree looks like it's about a hundred years old," she explained, "but the swing doesn't. Someone carved the name 'Margaret' on the seat. It seemed sad somehow," Annie said, remembering the swing. "I meant to ask you about it before now but kept forgetting. The other day when I was out with Daisy, I came across it again, and the oddest thing happened. Arvin Sturgis was sitting under the tree, and I swear he was talking to the swing."

"I suppose in a way he was," Lillian said with a hint of sadness in her voice. "Margaret was his daughter," Lillian explained, "his only child. She would be a few years older than you, I suppose. She was an adorable little girl, full of spirit and life. I never did hear what happened between her parents," Lillian continued, "but her mother took her away just before she was to start school and never came back. Mr. Sturgis hasn't been the same since that day. He keeps to himself, and I don't think anyone really knows what happened."

"That's terrible," Annie said. "I can't imagine losing a child like that. I'll bet that was her swing," Annie thought aloud. "He disappeared so quickly when he heard us approaching that I didn't even have a chance to speak to him."

"I'm sure that was his choice," Betty Lou told Annie. "He always did keep to himself, even as a child," Betty Lou remembered. "After Charlene left with Margaret, he barely spoke at all. At least not to anyone I knew. It was a big mystery for a long time, what happened to them. The police even looked into it but discovered they left voluntarily, and Arvin didn't try to fight her in custody. Hard to imagine, letting go of your only child."

"I met him once," Annie said thoughtfully in the hardware store about a week after I moved here. I heard his name and realized he must be my neighbor so, I stopped him to introduce myself. He grunted something about grandma's passing and then he was out the door. I haven't spoken to him since. I got the distinct impression that he was not open to a neighborly chat. Now I understand why," Annie said thoughtfully. "I suspect me being near Margaret's age doesn't help."

"I don't think he means to be rude," Betty Lou said kindly. "I think he's just been alone so long now that he doesn't remember how to talk to people."

"And you probably surprised him," Winnie added. "I don't suppose he expected to see anyone out in those woods."

"Well, I'll do my best to steer clear of that area from now on. I sure don't want to trespass or give him any reason to keep his distance."

"Well, that's settled then," Lillian said with a nod at the ladies. "Now where are those mint juleps? I'm parched!"

They all smiled at Lillian's affected Southern drawl, and thoughts of Arvin Sturgis were forgotten as soon as their drinks arrived.

22

Arvin Sturgis pushed his way through the low branches that for years had kept his favorite fishing hole away from uninvited hikers and fishermen alike. It was quiet and secluded. And it was his favorite spot in the world.

"Hey! What are you doing here?" Arvin shouted angrily at the young boy standing near the water's edge. This is my fishing hole, and I don't appreciate it!"

"Aah!" the boy yelled with surprise, instinctively turning toward and backing away from the man who had appeared suddenly from the thicket behind him. The rest of Arvin's rant was drowned out by a loud splash as the boy slipped on the muddy embankment and unable to get a foothold, slid quickly into the water.

Ryan Walsh flailed helplessly as he slipped through the long grasses at the edge of the creek, struggling to find something to grab onto.

With a speed that belied his age, Arvin Sturgis closed the gap between himself and the boy. Grabbing Ryan by his arms, the older man pulled him quickly out of the water and onto the grassy embankment.

Arvin Sturgis, who a moment ago had been in a rage, knelt on the ground trying to catch his breath. It had all happened so fast.

"Thank you," Ryan said shakily as he turned to look at the man who had pulled him to safety. "My name's Ryan," he said slowly, looking at the older man tentatively. "Remember? I brought you Christmas dinner from Annie next door?"

"I know who you are. What are you doing here?"

"Fishing," Ryan answered slowly, a bit confused by the question. They looked at each other for a long moment, and then the older man just turned to leave.

"Wait! Where are you going? Don't you want to fish?"

"Not anymore," Arvin said brusquely. "You ruined any chance I had of catching a fish with all that yelling and rolling around in the mud. If there were any fish around, they're long gone by now.

"Well, if you hadn't yelled at me, I wouldn't have disturbed your precious fish!" Ryan countered, feeling bold and a little hurt that this man didn't seem to like him. Arvin didn't bother to turn around.

Ryan knew the man was right; the fish was long gone by now. He headed home, thinking he'd have to find another place to fish or risk running into that nasty old man again. As he made his way through the field and came within sight of Annie's house, he heard a familiar voice call out to him.

"You're supposed to bring the fish out of the water, not go in after them!"

Ryan looked up, smiled, and ran across the backyard when he heard Pete Reed's voice calling out to him.

"Grandpa!" Ryan called as he ran toward the older man, jumping into his outstretched arms.

"So," Pete said as he picked the boy up and crushed him in a bear hug, "are we having fish for lunch?"

"No," Ryan said dejectedly, telling his grandpa about his encounter with Mr. Sturgis.

"Well, we'll just have to find you a better fishing spot while I'm here. Then maybe I can show you how to fish from the bank," he said with a wink. "For now, let's get you dried off, and then you can show me around the place."

23

"Two peas in a pod," Mary said, watching her husband with his new grandson. She and Annie watched the reunion through the kitchen window.

"I'm so glad you're here," Annie told her mother, giving her a quick hug, "for me, for Ryan, and Tom." He's looking forward to spending time doing guy stuff with Dad."

"Well, your dad will be in heaven then. I hope you were able to find something for him to do while we're here. I'm trying to get him to slow down a bit and take it easy, but he doesn't want any part of that."

"Is he okay?" Annie asked her mother, concern creeping into her voice. "What? Oh yes, he's fine. There's nothing to worry about Annie, really.

I just meant that he's been working for so long, and I want him to find some hobbies that he can focus on that really make him happy."

"Are things okay with the business? Is he unhappy there?"

"No, nothing like that. I probably shouldn't have said anything," Mary fretted. "It's just that the business is doing really well, but it's taking him out of the field more and more. You know how much he likes to be in the thick of things. Putting him behind a desk is like putting him in a box. He's restless."

"Annie, I'm wet," Ryan announced as he and his grandpa came through the side door into the mudroom, unknowingly interrupting their conversation.

"I'll say," Pete added. "We need to get him dried off and into some dry clothes."

"Okay, you know the drill," Annie said to Ryan. "Dirty clothes right into the washer, your socks and shoes too. There's a towel on the hook by the door," Annie said over her shoulder as she headed up the back stairs. "And I'll be right down with clean clothes."

As Ryan changed, Annie joined her mom and dad at the kitchen table. Pete relayed Ryan's story about falling in the water and Arvin pulling him out.

"He's a strange man," Annie said, "but I don't think he's any danger to Ryan. I think he's just going to need some time to adjust to a curious, fun loving ball of energy moving in next door. After all, it's been quite some time since children have lived in this house."

"About twenty years or so," Mary said as she took her daughter's hand in hers. "It's time to change that," she added with a smile.

"Annie, I need shoes," Ryan called out from the mudroom. "They're in here," Annie replied from the kitchen. "Come say hello to your grandma."

"Hi, Grandma," Ryan said brightly as he hugged Mary. "Did you bring any cookies?"

"You know I wouldn't come empty-handed," she said as she uncovered the large platter on the table.

A moment later, they heard Tom return with the old truck. Pete and Ryan headed back outside, and the three of them walked purposely toward the barn.

"So how can I help?" Annie asked her mother when they were alone again.

"I honestly don't know," Mary told her daughter. "I just thought it was high time we came for a longer visit and since your dad was willing to take the time off, here we are."

"Well, if working with his hands is what Dad needs, I'm sure he'll get that here. Tom assured me that he has quite a list for them to choose from to keep busy."

"Will Tom be able to be around much while we're here?"

"He's not planning another trip for at least a month, so those two should get lots of quality time together. I know Tom is really looking to learning from Dad. Harrison is not the hands-on type when it comes to building or fixing things. Most of what Tom learned growing up was from the men Harrison hired."

"Well, he's in good hands," Mary assured her daughter. "That goes for Ryan as well," Annie said, pleased to see the three most important men in her life spending quality time together.

"Well, he's in good hands," Mary assured her daughter. "That goes for Ryan as well," Annie said, pleased to see the three most important men in her life spending quality time together.

24

"Daisy!" Ryan called out as he pushed through the underbrush. They had been exploring the far back area of the property when they discovered an old road. It looked like it had not been used in decades, but Ryan could still make out the path.

Daisy had been making her normal inspection of the surrounding area, diving into the underbrush and emerging several yards ahead of where she went in. She normally paced herself to match Ryan's speed, occasionally getting far enough ahead that she would run back to him for a pat on the head before running off again.

Today, however, she had disappeared around a bend in the old road he was following, and Ryan had lost sight of her.

"Daisy!" he called again, louder than the first time. "Daisy, come!" he ordered.

Ryan quickened his pace when he heard rustling in the bushes ahead of him.

"No matter how hard you try girl, you're never going to catch that rabbit. Trust me. They are way too fast for you," he said good-naturedly as he stepped into the brush on the side of the old road. He could hear crashing and whining now, about thirty feet ahead of him. Ryan was about to call out to his dog again when he heard someone cry out in fear.

"Aaah! No! Get off me! Get off!"

Ryan began to run toward the sound. "Hey, girl, what have you got there?" he asked when he discovered Daisy standing over a boy who was lying on his right side, curled into the fetal position.

"Get him off me!" the boy cried. "Get him off!"

"Daisy, leave it," Ryan ordered, and the dog responded, walking to him and sitting at his feet. "Good girl, Daisy," he said, patting the dog's head. "Now stay."

Daisy remained seated as Ryan walked toward the boy who had scurried away and was trying desperately to stand up. Ryan could tell that he was hurt when he favored his left knee.

"Wait, let me help you," Ryan said to the boy. "You shouldn't put weight on that leg until you know for sure it isn't broken."

The boy had crawled to a nearby tree and was just pulling himself up when Ryan reached him.

"I'm sorry Daisy scared you," he said gently. "She would never hurt you."

When the boy didn't respond, Ryan knelt to get a closer look at his knee.

"It's pretty scraped up, but I think it will be okay. You just need to get it cleaned up." When he looked up, he saw the lines on the boy's face where he had wiped away his tears. Ryan didn't know if Daisy had made him cry or if he was crying when Daisy found him.

"Why don't we go to my house and my mom can clean that up for you?"

"No!" he answered quickly.

"Are you sure? We don't live too far from here, and I'll bet my dad would give you a ride home."

"No," the boy said again. "I've got to go." "Wait, my name's Ryan. What's yours?" "TJ," the boy replied.

"You new here?" "No, you?"

"Sort of," Ryan replied. "I moved here last year and live in the town with my dad. He and Annie are getting married when I get out of school. After that, we'll be living here in her house."

"Cool," TJ said.

"Yeah, this is Daisy. She's Annie's dog, but she likes me so she's kind of my dog too."

"She sure is friendly," TJ said, still a little apprehensive from her earlier greeting. He reached out his hand slowly to pet her head as she remained seated next to Ryan.

"Yeah, she likes to chase rabbits," Ryan said as Daisy sat with her nose in the air, searching for their scent. "She isn't fast enough to catch them so she can't hurt them. Go on Daisy," he said loudly and pointed in the direction she was sniffing. "Go get it!"

The large dog wasted no time diving into the woods and disappearing from view. There was no masking the noise she made, though, as she lumbered through the underbrush, clearly on the scent of one or more innocent rabbits. "What are you doing out here?" Ryan asked as he looked around."

"I like to climb this tree and sometimes I even swing if it's really hot. You know, just to cool down. I don't usually swing. It's for babies."

"I know what you mean. I haven't been swinging since I was a little kid. But it sure was fun then. Maybe you should sit down on the swing and rest your knee for a while. It's scraped up pretty bad."

"Aw, it's not so bad," TJ said, limping noticeably as he made his way around the tree. "But I think I will, just to be safe."

Ryan went the other direction and reached out to hold the swing for his new friend. When he did, he noticed the name "Margaret" was carved into it. "Hey, that's my first mom's name," Ryan said. "But everyone called her Maggie."

"Your first mom?" TJ asked.

"My real mom," Ryan said slowly. "But she's in heaven now. She was sick for a long time, and then she went to heaven."

"My mom's in heaven too," TJ said softly. "She wasn't sick though. She was in a car accident."

Neither boy said another word for a long moment as they stood there looking at the swing.

Had they looked up, they might have caught a glimpse of the older man slipping quietly away, tears running freely down his weathered face. After all, Arvin Sturgis had just learned that his only child was gone forever. Sometime later that night, when he was able to think past the heartache, he would realize that he now had a grandson who would soon be living right next door.

Daisy circled back around a short time later, and the boys said their goodbyes. They made plans to meet up again as soon as they could and then headed their separate ways.

"Let's go home, Daisy," Ryan said as Daisy took off in the direction they had come. Ryan followed as closely behind her as he could since he didn't know where he was. They had been on an old road when he ran into the woods after Daisy, but he wasn't exactly sure how to get back to that road or their property.

Daisy paused often to keep Ryan in sight. When they finally reached the old road they'd been following when Daisy had ducked into the underbrush, the dog instinctively turned to the left to continue on their walk.

"This way, Daisy," Ryan said. "We need to go home now. Maybe we'll come back tomorrow to see what else is out there."

Daisy circled around and headed back the way they'd come, weaving back and forth down the old road and back into familiar territory.

25

"What are you working on in your clubhouse?" Annie asked Tom and Pete during dinner. They had been spending a lot of time over the past week holed up in the barn with the front doors closed. Ryan had even made a sign for the door that said "No girls allowed."

Tom and Pete looked at each other, laughing at the clubhouse reference. "The sign was Ryan's idea," Tom informed her.

"And we thought it was perfect," Pete added, finishing Tom's thought. The two men went back to their dinners, completely evading Annie's question.

"So you're not going to tell us?" Annie said to Tom and her father. "Tell you what, sweetheart?" Tom asked, feigning ignorance.

"What you and Pete are doing in the barn all day every day," Mary said to Tom, looking back and forth between him and Pete.

"Sorry," Tom replied jovially. "Clubhouse rules." "Yep," Annie said to her mother. "Two peas in a pod."

"Son," Tom said as he noticed Ryan wasn't joining in the laughter around the table, "something on your mind?

"What do you mean?" Ryan asked as he looked up from his plate to find everyone at the table looking at him expectantly.

"You know you can talk to us, right?" "Sure, Dad, I know."

"Did you run into that mean old man again?" Pete asked his grandson. "The one from the fishing hole last week?"

"What? Oh no. I haven't seen Mr. Sturgis. But I did meet someone new today. A boy named TJ."

"Is he known in your class?" Annie asked.

"No, he's not in my class," he said casually as he took a mouthful of mashed potatoes.

"Then how did you meet this boy?" Tom asked, confused by Ryan's response.

"Daisy knocked him down," Ryan answered, taking another mouthful of potatoes.

"I think we're going to need a little more than that, Ryan," Tom said as he put his fork down and looked at Annie.

"Did she hurt him, Ryan? If Daisy hurt TJ, we need to call his parents right away."

"He's okay. He just scraped his knee when she knocked him over. I think she scared him since she's so big. I tried to get him to come home with me to have you fix it up for him, but he said no."

"Where were you when you ran into him?"

"Just taking a walk up the old lane out back," he told his dad. "Daisy and I like to take walks in the woods. Well, I like to walk in the woods. Daisy likes to chase rabbits," he explained with a grin.

"Well, next time you see him, be sure to tell him we'd love to meet him and his parents. They must live pretty close by for him to be in those woods," Annie mused.

"Okay, I'll tell him, but it might be just his dad. He told me that his mom's in heaven too."

The adults stole glances at each other as Ryan quickly finished his dinner.

"May I be excused?" he asked politely.

"Sure," Tom replied. "Just as soon as you carry your dishes to the kitchen and rinse your plate. Then why don't you come down to the barn with me and I can show you how our project is coming along."

"What project is that, Ryan?" Annie asked with a twinkle in her eye as she looked directly at Tom.

"Sorry, Annie, It's a secret," Ryan replied without a second thought.

Tom chuckled as Ryan headed into the kitchen "Nice try, Annie. Did you forget whose idea it was to make the sign?" Tom picked up his plate and followed his son out of the dining room, leaving Pete and the gals, as Pete referred to his wife and daughter, to clean up the kitchen.

As Pete helped put the food away, he asked Annie about her neighbor Arvin Sturgis. He knew the man lived next door as Annie had sent Ryan over with a plate of Christmas dinner when they were visiting last year. He just hadn't heard any more about him until Ryan relayed his story about running into him at the fishing hole the day he and Mary had arrived.

Annie filled in the blanks for her parents as best as she could and, in the process, realized she knew very little about the man. Only what Lillian had told her about his wife leaving and taking his daughter with her.

"I've lived here over a year now, and I have only seen him once at the hardware store in town. Now I find out that Ryan has seen him at least twice, once on Christmas day and then at the fishing hole. The man sure does like his privacy."

"Like someone else we know?" Mary asked her husband with raised eyebrows and a small grin.

"Uh, I need to, uh, go help Tom with something," Pete said hastily as he grabbed his jacket and headed out the door.

"That was smooth," Annie said, smiling at her mother.

26

"Cool," Ryan said as he stepped through the trees and looked at the old house. He had seen something from the road he and Daisy had been exploring and now he realized it was the roof of a house that had been almost completely hidden by the overgrown shrubs and trees that surrounded it. If he hadn't paused to catch his breath at the top of that last rise, he probably would have missed it completely.

Daisy came running up behind him and kept going right up the porch steps. She paced back and forth exploring the front porch, unable to find a way into the house. The retriever had a great nose and began whining and scratching at the bottom of a door located on the left side of the wide verandah.

"What is it, girl?" Ryan asked Daisy as he headed toward her. Daisy had stopped her pawing and seemed to be waiting for him to open the door and let her inside. He tried the handle and pushed the door several times, but it would not budge.

"It's locked," he said aloud. He stood on his toes and stretched to reach the small windows high up on the center of the door. Holding both hands up to cup his eyes, he tried to make out what was on the other side of the door. He could not make out anything. It was hard to tell if it was a lack of light inside or a covering on the window.

"Let's see if there is another way in."

They had almost completed their search around the building when Daisy discovered a basement window partially hidden by overgrown shrubs. Someone had cut the screen around the bottom so it appeared to be intact but was hanging in the frame like a curtain. When Ryan pulled the screen back, he found the window unlocked.

Ryan pulled his small flashlight out of his back pocket and realized he was looking into the basement of the old house. The large furnace was directly below the window and what appeared to be a canning cellar was across the large room on the right. He could make out a few old canning jars on various shelves, seemingly covered in grime.

The window was large for a basement window and Ryan was able to step directly onto the old furnace and then walk down a ramp that had been built beside it, probably for access to the oil filling mechanism on the top. That would also explain the large basement window and the location near the driveway. His dad had told him about the old oil heating systems when he was working in the basement in Eva's house. They had used hers on those cold days when the fireplace just wasn't enough to warm the house.

When Ryan reached the basement floor, he turned to call Daisy inside. He could no longer see her outside the window and then realized she was already beside him. She looked up at him as if to say "Okay, what are we waiting for?"

"I should have known," he said to her, shaking his head. They walked around the basement, exploring every corner and shelf. There were all sorts of old tools still hanging on the wall over the workbench in the corner, and there was even an old chest freezer lying on its side with the top open like a porch. As Ryan bent down with his flashlight to look inside, Daisy barked once and took off for the canning cellar.

"Daisy, no!" Ryan shouted as he heard the familiar sound of TJ trying to get Daisy off of him.

"What are you doing here?" Ryan asked when he found Daisy licking TJ's face as he huddled under the shelving in a corner of the small room. TJ didn't answer right away. He was getting a very thorough face-licking from his new friend Daisy, and this time, he just gave up trying to get her off. He seemed to actually be enjoying the attention.

"Okay, Daisy, that's enough," Ryan said, pulling her off the smaller boy. "I think he's clean enough for now," he said, smiling. He reached his other hand out to the boy to help him off the floor.

"Why were you hiding?" Ryan asked.

"I don't want to get in trouble," TJ answered honestly. "I don't think I'm supposed to be in here."

"Well, it doesn't look like anyone else is using this house at the moment.

How long have you been coming here? How's your knee?"

"Are you going to tell your dad?" TJ asked hesitantly. "What? I don't know. Why?" Ryan answered, not sure why the boy seemed scared of his father. "Do you know my dad? I really don't think he'd be mad," Ryan continued, still a little confused by TJ's response.

"No, but he might tell my dad, and then, I'd get in big trouble." "Why would you get in trouble?" Ryan asked. "Oh," Ryan said suddenly, "did you run away? Is that why you're afraid of your dad finding out? Are you hiding out here?"

"Not really," TJ replied slowly, clearly unwilling to share too much with his new friend no matter how nice Ryan was treating him.

"Then why?"

"Can you just not tell him?" TJ responded. "I swear I'm not doing anything bad. I don't want my dad to know where to find me."

Ryan wanted to know more about his new friend, but he decided to let it go. After all, TJ was the only boy near his age that Ryan had met at Annie's house, and he didn't want to push him away.

"Okay," he said finally. "I won't tell." "Thanks, Ryan," TJ said. "I owe you."

"Nah, we can call it even if you show me around the place." "Deal," TJ agreed quickly. "Follow me!"

For the next half hour, TJ showed Ryan around the old house as if it were his own. He told him how he'd found the house when he was walking through the woods, much like Ryan had but from the other direction. He didn't go into detail about where he lived, and he would either change the subject or just not answer when Ryan asked him questions about his home and family.

"I've got to go," TJ said suddenly as he looked out the attic window and noticed that it had started getting dark.

"Me too," Ryan said. "Annie will worry if I'm late for dinner. I'm staying with her and Daisy while my grandparents are here."

"Can you come back tomorrow?" TJ asked his new friend. "I won't be able to come tomorrow, but I can come back after church on Sunday." "Okay, see you Sunday. Bye, Daisy!" TJ yelled. Already heading into the underbrush, getting her head start on Ryan.

27

"You've been spending a lot of time in the woods lately," Tom said as he and Pete were sanding the final coat of lacquer on the new blanket chest they'd made as a gift for Annie. "What have you been doing out there?"

"Just exploring and stuff," Ryan said, hoping his dad didn't ask too many questions. "There are lots of old trees that were knocked down and big rocks that I can climb on."

"Sounds like fun! Have you seen that boy TJ lately?" "Um, just once, since I met him."

"How did he do with Daisy this time?"

"Oh, he's fine with her," Ryan said, realizing that his dad was still worried that Daisy had hurt the other boy. "They're friends now. I think she just scared him when she knockdown. She licks his face now, and he likes it."

"Do you know his last name?" "No."

"Well, next time you see him, why don't you invite him to come over so I can meet him? I like to know who your friends are, son."

"Okay, I'll try," Ryan replied. "I'm going to go inside now. Annie said I could help Grandma Reed make cookies." With that, he was gone.

"You worried about him?" Pete asked his future son-in-law.

"Not exactly," Tom said as he continued to work. "It just seems a little odd that he doesn't talk about this boy more. You'd think that if he made a new friend that lives close by, he'd be telling me all about him."

"Maybe he will when he's ready. You did say that he's only met this boy twice and the first time didn't go so well with Daisy. Maybe they aren't at the buddy stage yet."

"I guess I can't imagine anyone not wanting to be friends with Ryan. He's so outgoing and genuine." "That he is," Pete agreed.

"Then again I'm probably biased," Tom admitted with a grin. "Then that makes two of us, Tom."

"Was there anything, in particular, you'd like to do while you're here?" Annie asked her mother. They were sitting on the front porch swing, watching as Pete was attempting to teach Ryan and Tom how to whistle. "I'm doing it, honey," she said as she patted her daughter's leg. "I just want to spend time with you."

"And you know I love having you here. I worry that you'll be bored when I have to spend time at the shop. Of course, you're welcome to come with me whenever you'd like. I get pretty busy sometimes and don't want you to feel neglected."

"Now, don't you worry about me, Annie. You do what you need to do, and your dad and I will get along just fine. We knew before we came that you both had jobs and Ryan would be in school. It's just good for us to be here and for your dad to take some much-needed time off. We'll be fine, really."

"You forget how well I know you, Mom," Annie said, smiling. "I know you can't sit still. So that means you'll be cleaning and ironing and cooking and taking care of all of us while you're here. When do you get time off?" "Now that you mention it, I wouldn't mind seeing if any of my old friends were still around. I saw several at your grandma's service and, since we'll be coming back here more often now, it might be nice to reconnect with a few."

"Now that sounds like a great idea. I usually drive the truck to the shop so you and Dad can use my car anytime you'd like."

"How is the visit with your folks going?" Becca asked as she flipped through the skirts on the sale rack at the boutique down the street from

Annie's shop. Becca had arranged to take Annie out for a long lunch and catch up on their lives. "It's great having them here," she said honestly. "I do miss having them around. It's not ideal for them to stay with me since I'm not home all day and, Ryan is in school, but I think they're enjoying themselves."

"I'm sure they are. You said they have your car to get out and about and, they did use to live here. I suspect they'll want to take a ride now and then to explore their old hometown."

"Mom did say that she might try to reconnect with a few of her old friends. You know, since they'll be coming back here more often now."

"That's encouraging," Becca commented as she moved to an adjacent rack to continue her search for just the right piece. "Tom has been great about them being here too. We hardly have any time to ourselves now since they are staying with me, but he manages to find opportunities to get us alone for a little while almost every day. He's quite crafty about it too." Annie smiled as she remembered some of the situations Tom created to get her alone.

"He's smart, he's in love, and therefore he's highly motivated," Becca rationalized.

That he is, Annie thought to herself, remembering earlier that morning when Tom had asked her to meet him in the greenhouse. Their stolen moments were quite exhilarating, she decided, smiling at the memory.

"What would you think about us moving back here?" Pete asked his wife. They were in an old diner in a neighboring town that they hadn't visited since they'd moved away.

"Are you serious, Pete?" Mary asked her husband, clearly surprised by the suggestion.

"What if I were? Would you be okay with that?"

"I'd be in heaven, honey! I miss her so much. And now that she's starting a family, I don't want to miss a minute of it."

Pete just looked at his smiling wife for a moment as the waitress served their lunch.

"What about the company?" she asked him seriously when they were alone. "I didn't think you were ready to give it up yet."

"I didn't think so either until we came back this time. I think about how much I enjoy being with Tom and Ryan and the opportunity I have to teach them both all the things I know about building and fixing things…"

"About being a great husband and father…" Mary interjected.

"And being a granddad to a wonderful boy who is full of questions and eager to learn."

"And, God willing, there will be more grandchildren someday for you to love and teach."

"From your lips to God's ears, Mary," Pete said to his wife.

28

"We were surprised to see your neighbor Arvin Sturgis at Ryan's game today," Pete said to Tom. "I didn't think he was one to socialize."

"To my knowledge, he isn't," Tom replied, confused by what the older man was telling him. "I've never seen him there before," he continued. "Are you sure it was him?"

"It's been a long time," Mary Reed answered, "But it was Arvin Sturgis. He was sitting by himself on the bottom bleachers of the other team. I never saw him talk to anyone, but I noticed he did watch closely when Ryan was playing. He'd get a real good look at him from there since Ryan was playing first base. Do you think that's why he was there?"

"I honestly have no idea," Tom replied. "I'll have to ask Ryan and Annie if they've talked to him or seen him there before today."

"You never know," Pete said casually. "Maybe he's warming up to the idea of having neighbors. Ryan is a great kid."

"Thanks," Tom replied, "he sure is. Not that I can take credit for that, but I'm proud of him just the same."

"Let's go!" Ryan called to them from the barn. Annie had pulled the truck out and had set up lawn chairs in the back for her, Tom, and Ryan to sit on.

"Heads up, Dad," Annie called as she tossed her father the truck keys. "I thought you and Mom might like to do the honors."

"Sure, sweetheart. Just make sure you're safe back there."

"Once a parent, always a parent," Mary smiled and said to her daughter as she climbed into the cab of the truck beside her husband.

"I think we're both finding out what that means," she said to Tom as he helped her into the bed of the truck. Ryan had begged to ride in the back on the way to Betty Lou's house for dinner, and Tom had agreed on one condition. They set up the lawn chairs, and Ryan sat in the middle. There was no way he was letting his son sit on the outside as they drove into town. It wasn't far, but it wasn't exactly legal either.

"What a beautiful night," Annie said to Tom as they drove slowly along the back roads into town.

"I love the weather here," Tom replied. "Not too much cold during the winter but just enough to enjoy it. And here we are in the middle of April riding in the back of a truck and it's balmy."

"Better than Seattle" Annie exclaimed with a grin. "But I thought San Francisco had perfect weather."

"That's San Diego," he told her. "San Francisco is great, but it can be chilly, even in summer. Besides, no matter how good the weather is, it has a long way to go to beat Magnolia Creek."

Sunday after church, Annie announced that she was going to visit Lillian at Magnolia Lane.

"Ryan, would you like to go with me? I'm planning to stop by the shop first to pick up some fresh cut flowers for Eva. Lillian said at church today that her roommate has not been feeling well and could use the cheering up. I know she'd love to see you too."

"Can I go after school tomorrow instead? I sort of told TJ that I would see him this afternoon."

"Of course, honey. I'll kiss her for you and tell her you'll be stopping by to see her soon. Just make sure your dad knows where you're going to be since I won't be here." Ryan and Daisy arrived at the old house first, and Ryan made himself at home. TJ had shown him everything that he had already explored, but there was plenty more to discover. His new friend had rigged a hammock on the back porch out of an old blanket and rope he'd found in the cellar. After exploring the inside of the house further, he began to look around outside while he waited for his new friend. The old barn did not fare as well as the house after years of neglect.

A large portion of the roof and the back of the hayloft had fallen in and were blending into the weeds and brush growing through the barn floor. He decided to wait for TJ before exploring the inside.

It turned out he had a long wait. After several hours of exploring the house and napping in his friend's hammock, Ryan and Daisy headed back to Annie's house.

"We'll come back tomorrow after school," he told Daisy as they made their way back to the road.

They were on their way back to the church for pizza after the baseball game, and Tom was taking back roads since several of the boys were riding in the back of the truck.

"You know, that's the second time Arvin Sturgis has been at the ball field," Tom said to Annie.

"At Ryan's game?" she asked him, surprised by his statement. "Yes." Tom nodded slowly. "Your mom and dad thought they saw him in the visitor stands at the last game, but I didn't think to mention it to you before now. Honestly, I thought the odds were so slim that it was him that I didn't think of it again until today. When I was coaching third base, I was close enough to see him. He avoided eye contact with me the entire inning. By the time we were at bat again he was gone. I don't know if he left the game or just moved out of my sight, but I didn't see him again. I looked for him as we were rounding up the boys but didn't see him or his truck in the parking lot."

"You're sure it was him?" Annie asked, still skeptical. Hiding from them didn't surprise her at all; just the fact that he would even go.

"Oh, it was Arvin all right. And it's a start," he said with satisfaction, turning to smile at Annie. "It's a start. Maybe one of these days he'll speak to us," he added with mock surprise.

"Now, don't go getting your hopes up, Tom Walsh. He's not the type to swap stories over the fence."

Tom laughed at the mental picture and was about to respond when something hard hit the back window of the truck, catching him by surprise. He quickly turned his attention to the boys in the back, slowing down instinctively as he did so.

"Sorry Dad!" Ryan yelled to be heard through the glass. The boys had been goofing around, burning off some energy after their big win. Tom didn't blame them; they'd worked hard and deserved to enjoy themselves. He'd just prefer it didn't cost him a new window.

They arrived at the church moments later, thoughts of Arvin Sturgis temporarily forgotten.

"I can't believe it's time for you to leave. It seems like you just got here," Annie said as she hugged her parents in turn. "I know, honey, but we'll be back before you know it.

After all, the wedding is only two months away! And we'll talk on the phone whenever we can."

"I know," Annie replied with a forced smile. "It's just that I've gotten pretty used to you being around. I'm going to miss you is all."

"Me too, sweetie, more than you know."

"Okay, you two, my turn," Pete said as he stepped up beside Annie, waiting for his turn to hug his daughter good-bye. By the time Mary was done hugging Tom and Ryan, she wiped furiously at her tears.

"It's okay to cry," Pete told his wife as they headed into the airport. "It just means you have a big heart."

"You old softie," she said, smiling at her husband as he put his arm around her. "You're going to miss them too."

"I sure am," Pete admitted softly, giving his wife another squeeze before they headed toward the plane that would take them across the country, away from their only daughter and her new family.

29

It has been almost a week, and the note that Ryan left for TJ on the second day was still tucked under the old coffee can that sat on the kitchen table. He was sure that TJ had not been there or he would have found the note.

He was thinking about what to do when he heard the basement window slide open. Daisy began a low growl just as Ryan heard slow, heavy footsteps on the basement stairs. He tried hard to keep Daisy quiet, but she was aware of someone approaching and would not settle down.

Ryan stepped out of sight around the corner in the kitchen just as the door to the basement opened.

As the figure stepped into the kitchen, Daisy jumped out of Ryan's hand and headed straight for it with a single bark.

"Hey, girl," TJ said as he knelt to pet her head. "Where's Ryan?"

"What happened?" Ryan asked as he stepped into the kitchen and saw the bruising on TJ's arm and face. "Are you okay?" His friend looked like he'd been in a fistfight and had not fared well.

"Yeah, I'm okay," TJ said. "It looks worse that it feels. So what have you been up to?"

"TJ, what's going on? You've been gone for days, and now you look like you've been in a fight. What happened?"

"Oh, I did something stupid and got in trouble," he said in an offhand manner, smiling on the side of his face that was not still swollen. Ryan could see that the effort was painful.

"That looks bad, TJ. Did you go to school? What did the nurse say?"

"It's all over now, and I don't want to talk about it, okay? Can we just have some fun before I have to go?"

"Sure," Ryan said, unconvinced that his friend was okay. He looked pretty banged up.

As they explored the upstairs of the house, TJ showed Ryan all the little hiding places he had found or made since he'd been coming to this old house.

"I've got stuff stashed all over here," TJ announced proudly. "What kind of stuff?" Ryan asked.

"I've got food, water and sodas," TJ began, counting the items off on his fingers, "paper and pens, playing cards, and I even have toilet paper!"

"Wow," Ryan said, impressed with the older boy. "How long have you been coming here?"

"Not long," TJ answered. "When I first found this place, it was still pretty cold out, so I couldn't stay for long. I did find an old blanket in the barn, but I don't go out there anymore."

"How come?"

"It's too dangerous. I'm pretty brave," TJ assured the younger boy, "but it's falling, and I don't want to get trapped in there. Who would ever find me?"

"Well, can you show me the part you did go into? I just want to look inside. I promise I won't go in there when you're not here."

"I guess that would be okay, but I'm older so you have to do what I say, ok?"

"Sure," Ryan responded, happy to be getting a peek inside the old barn. He eagerly followed his friend across the backyard, Daisy at his side "Arvin?" Tom called out as he neared the older man. Tom had spotted him in the parking lot of the local home and garden store. Startled, Arvin Sturgis turned around quickly toward the sound of Tom's voice. When he spotted Tom, he hurried his steps toward his truck, turning away from Tom without a word.

"Arvin, please stop," Tom said gently, quickly catching up to the man. "I just want to talk to you."

Arvin reached his truck and was about to climb in when Tom appeared beside him. As he reached for the door handle, Tom said, "Just give me two minutes, Arvin. Please."

The older man lowered his hand into his pocket but did not turn around.

"If you don't want to be friends, I can live with that. I understand that you're a private man. But we are going to be neighbors soon. Annie has agreed to marry me, so Ryan and I will be moving into her place after our wedding in June."

"You and Ryan" Arvin asked softly, clearly surprised by this news. "Yes," Tom replied. "We're all going to be neighbors, so I thought it would be a good idea to at least have a passing relationship." "Engagement," Arvin said softly, remembering Charlene's words the first time he'd heard her voice in nearly thirty years.

"Congratulations on your engagement," she'd said to Annie and Tom. "Goodbye, grandmother and grandfather," Ryan had called to them from the front porch. "Yes," Tom said again, assuming that Arvin was speaking to him. "Annie and I got engaged last Christmas, and we're getting married in June."

Arvin never said another word as he climbed into his truck and closed the door. A moment later, he was gone, and Tom had no idea what had just happened.

"That's far enough, Ryan," TJ told him as he ventured into one of the horse stalls near the front of the old barn. The front barn doors remained intact, although they hung askew across the front of what was left of the old building, providing just enough daylight to see about thirty feet into the structure.

"This is so creepy," Ryan said a moment later as he popped his head out of the stall, taking stock of the large entrance area of the barn. "Cool," Ryan said, "but creepy. Like, you can almost smell the hay and the animals, but there's mud and weeds everywhere."

"That's where I found the blanket," TJ told him. "In that stall you were just in. It was pretty wet and dirty, but it dried out okay when I hung it over a branch. It took about a week because it kept raining, but it did clean it off a little bit."

"Does it still stink?" Ryan asked.

"You tell me." TJ smiled. "You don't seem to have any problem sleeping on it."

"The hammock?" Ryan asked as it dawned on him what TJ meant. "Cool," he said with a smile. "Nope, doesn't stink at all now."

"So what's out back?"

"Lots of high grass and snakes, I guess. I haven't gone back there. I don't like snakes. Let's go back to the house before it starts to get dark," TJ said, turning toward the house.

"I don't mind snakes," Ryan said, looking longingly toward the back of the barn. "I even caught one with my bare hands before," he bragged, unaware that the older boy kept walking.

"C'mon, Ryan you promised to listen to me about the barn."

Ryan turned and ran to catch up with TJ, who was already halfway across the back yard.

"I spoke to Arvin today," Tom announced at the dinner table that evening. "I saw him in the parking lot at the home store and decided it was as good a time as any to introduce myself."

Annie put her fork back down on her plate and stared at him expectantly.

"And?" she prodded when Tom began eating again. "And I don't know," Tom said honestly. "I convinced him to give me a couple of minutes of his time, assured him that in no way was I interested in butting into his life but that we were going to be neighbors and I thought it was a good idea to at least be civil to each other. You know, a friendly nod when we pass each other is all I'm looking for."

"So how did he respond? Did he say okay or get away from me you weirdo or what?"

"He seemed preoccupied with our engagement," Tom told her, shrugging his shoulders as he did so.

"Why? What did you say to him?" Annie asked.

"I just told him that Ryan and I would be moving in here after the wedding in June. All he said was "engagement" and then he got in his truck and drove off.

"Engagement Very odd," Annie said. "But at least you made the effort. Thanks for trying."

30

"Hey buddy, what's up?" Chad said as he bounded up the front porch steps. Ryan had called him and asked him to come by after school. He needed to talk to someone about TJ, and he had promised the other boy that he wouldn't talk to his dad. He thought Chad would know what to do. "Can I talk to you about something? I promised my friend that I wouldn't tell my dad, but I'm worried about him." "Sure, Ryan, Let's take a walk."

As they walked around Annie's property, Ryan told him about meeting TJ and exploring in the woods. He told him about how TJ had not wanted his dad to find out that he had been coming to the old house.

"He even made me promise not to tell my dad about it, but I don't know why."

"Do you think he was doing something he shouldn't be while he was there?" Chad asked, praying the other boy was not exposing Ryan to drugs.

"Like what? He said he had just been hanging out there. He did build a cool hammock on the porch with some rope and an old blanket." Ryan smiled, remembering how it felt to lie there without a care in the world. "But he didn't steal anything or break anything."

"Do you have any idea why he was so afraid of you telling your dad about him?"

"Not really, but it seemed to me like he was afraid that my dad would tell his dad and he'd get in trouble. Boy," Ryan said, remembering how TJ looked the last time he saw him, "I sure wouldn't want to get in trouble with his dad either!"

"What makes you say that?" Chad asked, suspecting he'd hit on something important.

"Well, we agreed to meet after school, but he never showed up. That was three days ago. Yesterday he finally showed up, and he didn't look so good. He didn't want to talk about it, but he did tell me that he'd done something stupid and gotten in trouble."

"Ryan, what do you mean when you said he didn't look so good? Did he look sick or was he hurt?"

"His face and arm on the side were pretty banged up," Ryan said, indicating his left side. "He said it looked worse that it felt, but his face was all puffy. And he didn't use that arm much, so I think it did hurt. He just didn't want me to think he was a baby."

"I see," Chad said carefully. "And what's your friend's name?"

"TJ," Ryan replied, "but I don't know his last name. I don't think he goes to my school. I did ask him if the school nurse said anything about the bruises, but he didn't want to talk about it. Do you think he just stayed home from school?"

"He may have. The nurse would have asked about the bruises and may have even called his father about it. From what you've told me, he's afraid of his father hurting him if he gets in trouble again."

"I think so," Ryan said, looking at Chad with a worried expression.

"Well, you did the right thing coming to me, Ryan. Sometimes people need help even when they don't know it. I did, and your dad helped me, so I'm going to help you. Let me see what I can find out without getting him into trouble," Chad reassured him. "And in the meantime, if you see TJ again, try to see if he'll talk about his family at all. Does he have any brothers or sisters?"

"I do know his mom is in heaven," Ryan said helpfully. "She wasn't sick like my mom. She had a car accident."

"Whoever he is, he's lucky to have you for a friend, Ryan Walsh."

31

"I just miss him so much," Susannah confided in her mother over their weekly lunch at the country club. "I know he's where he belongs and that he's happy with Tom, but he'd been with me for so long that I think I Underestimated how big that hole in my heart was going to be when I left him there."

"I miss him too," Charlotte replied as their salads arrived, "but don't you think it's time you started living your own life? You've been filling in for your sister for so long now. It's time for you to think about starting your own family."

"Ryan is family," Susannah said emphatically, frustrated that her mother didn't appear to miss Ryan at all, despite what she said.

"You know that's not what I meant, Susannah. Don't twist my words. Of course, he's family. He's my grandson, and he's all I have left of Maggie," she said with a catch in her voice. "He's all any of us have left."

"I'm sorry, Mother. Perhaps it's time for a visit. Ryan will be getting out of school soon. Maybe he can come up here for a few days. I'm sure Annie and Tom are busy with plans for the wedding. They might appreciate a break!"

"That sounds wonderful, dear. We could plan a party with some of his old friends. How does that sound?"

"It sounds like my quality time with Ryan is going to turn into a social event," she said to her mother with a twinkle in her eye. It didn't matter, she thought. It'll make my mother happy, and all we have to do is show up and have fun. The rest of the time, he's all mine.

"He'll love it!" Tom told Susannah when she called to make the arrangements. "I'll have him call you back when he gets home. He's helping Annie deliver flowers, and they are usually-done before lunch. Better yet, I'll text you when he gets here then you can call and tell him yourself."

Tom sent Annie a text and asked her to call him when she had a minute. He wanted to make sure she hadn't planned anything else for Ryan that afternoon and to let her in on the plans.

"He's going to be so happy," Annie told Tom when he explained what Susannah had proposed. "He was talking about her this morning. He's mentioned her several times over the past couple of weeks. It seems like maybe he's missing her too."

"So it's settled," Tom told Annie later that day, after talking with Susannah for the second time. "She's planning to fly into Richmond, and I told her we'd bring Ryan up there on Friday. We need to have our tuxes fitted, so we can do that before I take him to the airport."

"Sounds like you have this all planned out," she said with a smile as she cleared the table from dinner.

"And then some," he added cheerfully. "I took the liberty of booking you a full spa package at that salon you and Becca like so much. Gina already agreed to work the entire day at the shop, so you're free. Susannah said she'd see you when she brings Ryan back and to have a marvelous time."

"How did I get so lucky?" she asked as she sat on Tom's lap and kissed him. A man who knows how to book a spa day is truly a rare find.

"Are you two kissing again?" Ryan asked with a sigh as he came down the stairs and into the kitchen.

"No, we were just..." Annie began as she stood up and turned toward Ryan.

"Yes, we were," Tom said happily, pulling Annie back down onto his lap. "But you don't have to watch. Don't you have homework to do?

"Nope, it's all done!" Ryan announced proudly.

"Well, I'm going to take my doggie and go home" she announced, once again standing up this time, bending down to kiss Tom good-bye. She encircled Ryan in her arms from behind and kissed his cheek loudly as he squirmed and laughed, loving the attention.

"Come, Daisy. Let's go home!"

Tom walked her out to the truck, opening the door for Daisy to climb in first. They made a plan for dinner on Tuesday after Ryan's baseball game, and Annie headed home.

32

"How are things, Ryan?" Chad asked as they left the café and headed toward the square in town.

"Good, but I haven't seen TJ since the last time we talked. I hope he's okay. Do you think he got in trouble again?"

"It's possible, but even if he did, you know it's not your fault, right?" "Sure, I didn't do anything wrong, did I? I mean, he wouldn't have gotten in trouble because of me, right?"

"No, you didn't do anything wrong, Ryan. Maybe he's just busy with school or chores," Chad said.

"Or maybe he just doesn't want to hang around with me." "I may suppose," Chad said, "but highly unlikely.

You're awesome, Ryan, and I love hanging out with you. So it's not you, okay? Are we clear on that?"

"Clear," Ryan answered, sitting up a little straighter. He looked up to Chad, and the compliment he just received from the older boy quickly dissolved his momentary insecurity. "So what do you think I should do?" "Well, I figured out who TJ is and who his family is. I have to be straight with you, Ryan. It's not good news." Ryan didn't respond, so Chad continued. "Do you remember that night last year when I got in trouble for breaking into Annie's store?"

Ryan just nodded his head, not sure where this was headed.

"Well, the older boy who stole the car and made us break into the shop is TJ's older brother."

"That's not good," Ryan agreed. "Could be the one who is hurting TJ? I thought you said he was in jail."

"He was in jail, but he isn't any more. He got out a few months ago. But no, I don't think he's the one hurting TJ. He didn't stay in town long when he got out. He had already dropped out of school, so when he got out of jail and came back here, his father kicked him out. I heard he moved away."

"I know he did some bad stuff, but why would his dad kick him out? He probably didn't have anywhere else to go.

Why would he do that?" Ryan asked Chad, trying to make sense of what he was just told.

"Unfortunately, not all dads are as great as yours, Ryan. Some are mean, some do things that hurt their kids, and some just leave. I think TJ's dad is the kind that hurt their kids."

"But why?" Ryan asked. "What did TJ do that was so bad?" "Absolutely nothing, Ryan It's hard to explain, but for men like that, they don't really need a good reason to hit. I remember when his brother used to come to school with bruises on his face and say that he got in a fight with an older kid and the other kid looked worse. Everyone believed him, and that's why he got into so much trouble. The truth was, his own father was hitting him."

"Is that going to happen to TJ too? Is he going to start doing bad things and go to jail like his brother?"

"I just don't know," Chad answered truthfully. "But I do know that someone needs to make him stop. It's against the law to beat up your kids. His father could go to jail. I know TJ doesn't want you to say anything, but someone has to stop his father from hurting him. Do you have any ideas about what we could do?"

"Well, he made me promise not to tell my dad, and I didn't. But maybe I should. I know TJ will be mad at me, but I don't want him to get hurt anymore. But if they put his father in jail, where will he live? He doesn't have a mom." Chad turned to look Ryan in the eye. "You trust me, right?"

"Yes," Ryan nodded. "What do you think I should do?"

"I'd like you to introduce me to TJ. If he will be my friend, I may be able to help him before he gets really hurt or starts doing bad things. I knew his brother, and I think I can help him. What do you think?"

"I think it's a good idea. You'll be a good friend for him and, you're helping me already."

"Great. I have one condition. If this gets bad, or if I think TJ is in any real danger, I'm going to tell the police. I think I can help him, but I can't risk him getting hurt again. Do you understand that? His father is a grown man and is a lot stronger than TJ. The next time he hits him, TJ might end up in the hospital."

"Agreed," Ryan told Chad. "When do you want to meet him?"

"You said that you and he have been fixing up the place a bit, right?"

"TJ did most of it before I got there, but yes, we've done as much as we can. Why?"

"Because I have tools," Chad said with a grin.

"I think you and TJ are going to get along just fine," Ryan said, thinking about, how much the boys could accomplish with the older boy's size and strength. Chad having his tools was a huge bonus!

"Then let's go by my house to pick up my tools, and I'll drive you over there. We can see if TJ is around and hopefully do a little work around the place before it gets dark."

33

"TJ, are you here?" Ryan called as he and Chad walked in the front door of the old farmhouse.

"Go find him, Daisy," Ryan said as he sent the dog to search for his friend. "He's usually always here on Sunday afternoons," Ryan explained to Chad.

When Daisy didn't come back right away, Ryan and Chad headed down to the basement where she had gone just moments before.

"Daisy where are you girl, did you find him?"

Daisy barked once and came bounding out of the root cellar. She got almost to Ryan and turned and headed back the way she'd come.

"TJ, are you in there? It's just me, Ryan." "Are you alone?" TJ asked timidly.

"I brought my friend Chad with me today so he can meet you and see the house. He's cool, you'll see. I think you'll like him. C'mon out."

TJ walked slowly out of the shadows of the root cellar, Daisy by his side. He kept the large dog between him and the stranger Ryan had brought with him.

"Hey, man, nice to meet you," Chad said, holding out his fist for the requisite bump. TJ touched his fist to Chad's in greeting but kept his distance.

"So what do you say we go back up into the light and get started?" Chad asked Ryan, motioning for TJ to join them. "Get started on what?" TJ asked Ryan as he followed his friend up the stairs.

"Chad's got tools!" Ryan exclaimed as he flashed TJ a grin.

"Sweet" TJ replied, thinking of what they could do around the place with actual tools.

"You guys are in charge," Chad said lightly, as he picked up his tool belt and fastened it around his hips, "and I'm all yours for the afternoon. Where do you want to start?"

As the boys talked about the projects they'd been thinking about, TJ relaxed noticeably around Chad, even joking with him on occasion.

Chad kept it casual, not mentioning anything about TJ's family or the yellowish marks on his arms and face that were the remnants of old bruises.

The younger boys learned how to fix the screen door that opened onto the front porch and replaced the missing latch so they could use it to let the breeze in.

They stood the refrigerator up and slid it back into its place beside the old stove, shored up the ceiling light fixture that was hanging by one side so they could now walk under it, and found enough pieces of wood to build a table and basic stools to put in the kitchen. At the end of the day, they sat at the table enjoying their snacks, appreciating all they had accomplished in just a few hours.

"I hope you'll let me come back again some time," Chad said to TJ and Ryan as they helped him pick up his tools. "I wouldn't mind giving that hammock a try next time. After we're done working of course,"

"Sure," TJ said enthusiastically, "that would be cool."

"Well, let me know when you're ready to do some more work. You can usually find me at the Victorian Café on the weekends. My mom runs the place, so I work there too. Stop by sometime when you're hungry, and I'll hook you up with the best cooking in town," he added proudly.

"Maybe I will," TJ said.

"You ready, Ryan? It's going to be dark pretty soon, and I know you need to get home."

"C'mon, Daisy, Let's go. Bye, TJ, see you later!"

"Bye, Ryan. Bye, Daisy. Bye, Chad!" TJ shouted as he slipped into the woods on the far side of the house.

"That went pretty well, don't you think?" Ryan asked Chad as they headed back down the path toward Annie's house.

"I do, indeed, He seemed a little unsure at first, but he warmed up to me pretty well, I think."

"I think so too. Thanks, Chad."

"That's what friends are for, buddy," Chad said as he took the extra tool bucket from Ryan, who was struggling under the weight of it, "To help share the load."

34

"*What is it about chocolate that brings such pure joy?* Annie thought. *From sweet and light to rich and dark, it just seems to fill a need.*"

And Annie had a need. She ripped open the bag of semisweet chocolate chips she kept in the cupboard for cookies and, in her haste, spilled a dozen or more on the counter. She quickly scooped them up and popped them all in her mouth at once. As she stood there in the kitchen savoring the chocolate melting in her mouth, she caught a glimpse of her reflection in the window over the sink. Even with the distortion of the glass, Annie could see the stunned look on her face.

She took a deep breath through her nose as she slowly swallowed the chocolate in her mouth. *You need to get a grip*, she thought as she stared at her reflection. She turned to sit down at the kitchen table in the middle of the large kitchen, taking a moment to compose herself.

"*What are the odds?*" Annie thought. "*No,*" "*What are the odds that Arvin Sturgis would be Ryan's grandfather?*" "*A million to one?*"

"*A billion to one?*" Annie didn't know whether to laugh or cry, so she did both.

Rising from the table, Annie hurriedly made the coffee she had excused herself to the kitchen to prepare. As she went through the motions, her mind raced at the absurdity of the situation and also the possibilities this revelation provided.

Ryan had a grandfather he never knew. But it was Arvin Sturgis.

She still couldn't wrap her head around the news that Arvin Sturgis, her standoffish neighbor, and confirmed recluse, was Maggie's biological father. That made Charlotte Davidson, queen of Philadelphia high society, Arvin Sturgis's runaway wife! Annie shook her head and laughed out loud at that realization. *"Well, this will certainly make for interesting family gatherings!"* Annie thought to herself.

And Ryan, He would have another insight into his mother that he never knew. Based on her brief encounter with Charlotte and Frederick at Christmas, Annie had no reason to expect that Charlotte ever spoke to anyone about her earlier life in Magnolia Creek, certainly not to her grandson.

"I can't wait to talk to the ladies," she thought, smiling as she contemplated the looks on their faces when she told them the news. She would definitely have to think of the best way to surprise them. This kind of opportunity didn't come along often.

With the coffee tray ready, Annie quickly wiped her moist eyes and dabbed at the chocolate remnants around the corners of her mouth with the dishtowel, pulling herself together before returning to the living room. This was going to be interesting to see where this was headed. After all, they were dealing with Arvin Sturgis.

"Arvin and I were just talking about Maggie," Tom informed Annie when she returned to the living room, sitting her tray down on the coffee table that currently separated the two men. Arvin seemed a bit more relaxed and thanked Annie for the coffee. He looked away quickly when she gave him an encouraging smile, but it was progress.

Arvin had not yet settled back into his chair, appearing ready to flee at the first sign of trouble. Tom also sat on the edge of his seat but for a different reason. Annie could see that Tom was intrigued and eager to hear Arvin's story. After all, he had married the man's daughter when they were both young and had only recently found out that he had a son. That son was the topic of the conversation at hand.

"If it's okay with you folks, I'd like to tell him myself," Arvin said, referring to his grandson Ryan.

Tom looked at Annie before answering, but she just nodded at him. As Ryan's father, this was his decision. Annie was confident he would make the right one for Ryan.

"Agreed," Tom told Arvin, "but with one condition. We need to give Frederick and Charlotte time to tell him that his mother was not Frederick's daughter, as far as he knows, Frederick is Maggie's father and his grandfather. I'll ask them to be sure to not discuss you with him, but prepare him for the news that he has another grandfather. They can explain that Maggie's real father, you, had no idea he even existed. When he returns from Philadelphia, you can tell him."

Arvin agreed with the plan, and they decided to give Ryan a week or two after he returned from visiting his family in Philadelphia to let their news settle in. Tom told Arvin he would let him know when he felt Ryan was ready.

35

"You're quiet, son something on your mind?" "No, just fishing."

"Okay, well, if that changes…" "Dad?"

"Uh-huh?"

"Is there ever a time when it's okay to break a promise?" "Are you thinking about breaking one now?"

"I don't know, maybe."

"Well, I think in a case like this, a man's got to follow his instincts. If you're even considering it, there is probably a good reason for it."

"It's just that things have changed, and I don't know if the promise even matters anymore."

"Do you want to tell me what it is and see if I can help you decide?" "That's just it, I can't tell you. That's the promise."

"TJ?"

"How'd you know?" Ryan asked, looking at his father for the first time since the conversation began.

"It wasn't too hard to guess. So, what do you want to do about it?" Tom asked, keeping his eyes on the water.

"I don't know," Ryan said dejectedly.

"Well, how about this? If no one is in danger, maybe you can take a little more time to think about it. Or maybe you can talk to someone else if you think that's allowed. Someone you trust like Annie or Grandpa Reed."

"That might work. I sort of already talked to Chad about it. That's one of the things that changed."

"I'm glad you felt comfortable going to Chad. He's a great guy. But if someone is in danger, I'd like you to tell me right now. You'll have a hard time living with the guilt, Ryan if you could have stopped someone from getting hurt but didn't do it. I want you to be sure before you wait."

"Okay, Dad. I'm going to think about it a little more." "Well, I'm glad that's settled then."

"Me too, Thanks, Dad." "Anytime son."

36

"Hi, Tom, What brings you by?"

"Have you got a few minutes for a chat?" Tom asked Chad. "Sure, let me just tell my mom I'm out here if she needs me," Chad said as he ran back into the kitchen of the café.

Tom took a seat on the back porch step while he waited for him to return.

"I brought you a sweet tea," Chad said as he handed Tom the glass of tea, taking a seat beside his mentor.

"Thanks. Chad, Ryan said he confided in you about TJ, but he's struggling with whether or not to talk to me about it."

"Ah," Chad said. "I'm glad he finally brought it up to you."

"I don't want him to break his confidences, but I'm a little concerned. That's why I wanted to talk to you, man to man."

"Of course, Tom whatever you want to know," Chad replied willingly. "First off, is he or anyone else in any danger?"

"Well, that's part of the problem," Chad began. "But I assure you it's not Ryan," he added quickly. "It's TJ that I'm worried about."

"How so?" Tom asked, leaning forward to encourage Chad to continue. "I think his dad's hitting him," Chad said solemnly.

"I see," Tom said, sitting back against the porch post. "Do you know why he didn't want Ryan to talk to me about him?"

"From what he's told me, he made him promise the first time they met that he wouldn't tell you because he was afraid that you might tell his dad. He's afraid of his dad and, from what I've seen, with good reason."

"What have you seen, Chad? Did you tell the authorities?" No, not yet.

By the time Ryan introduced me, TJ's bruises were almost all gone. I know from what my mom told me about my dad that they needed proof. I was concerned that the bruises were too old to count and that it would just make his dad mad. I didn't want him to get hurt worse."

"How bad was it? Could you tell?"

"No broken bones but, a lot of twisting bruises on his arm, and the side of his face was swollen like he'd either been hit with something flat or slammed against a wall."

"How long has it been since you've seen TJ?" Tom asked, immediately concerned for the young boy's welfare.

"I've seen him every day since Ryan introduced us a couple of weeks ago."

"Has he shown any further signs of abuse?"

"No, and believe me, I've been watching him closely."

"There's something else you should know," Chad continued as Tom considered what to do. "His older brother is the one who stole the car that night that we broke into Annie's shop."

37

"There she is," Tom pointed to Susannah as she walked toward them in the waiting area of the main airport terminal. She spotted Tom and waved as Ryan was already making his way to greet her.

"Mmm, I missed you, Ryan," Susannah said as she hugged Ryan tightly. "Nobody gives hugs as you do. You have a gift for it." She smiled as her nephew glowed with pride and hugged her more tightly as they walked back to where Tom was waiting. It was still a little strange to think of Ryan as her nephew when she had been his legal guardian and mother less than a year ago.

"Hello, Tom," she said as she hugged Ryan's father warmly. "Do you have time to grab a bite to eat? The flight back to Philadelphia doesn't board for another ninety minutes."

"That sounds great. Ryan, do I even need to ask if you're hungry?" Tom smiled at his son.

"Nope, I'm always hungry," Ryan replied cheerfully. They quickly agreed on a restaurant, placed their orders, and sat back to relax while they waited for the food.

"How is Annie holding up with all the wedding planning? She must be exhausted with the wedding less than a month away," Susannah asked Tom, who sat across from her in the booth. Ryan had opted to sit next to his aunt, and Tom could tell that pleased her greatly. She had told him many times that she did miss having him around all the time, but she knew the best place for Ryan was with his father. Tom understood but couldn't agree more with her decision.

"She's amazing," Tom said proudly. "She keeps the shop going, makes all the wedding decisions, and still finds time to make her deliveries to Magnolia Lane and visit with her friends. I don't know how she finds time for me and, Ryan but she does."

"Did she come with you today? You mentioned booking her a spa day." "She did," said Ryan quickly. "Well, almost all the way, anyway. And Aunt Becca came too. We dropped them off at the spa in Short Pump to get pampered. Then Dad and I went to the store to try on our tuxedos for the wedding."

"Scott has a meeting in Richmond today," Tom explained. "So he's going to have his last tux fitting later this afternoon, and then he'll bring the girls home."

"Well, I'll bet you both look handsome in your tuxedos," Susannah said to Ryan.

"We do," Ryan said, with not even a touch of humility. Tom caught Susannah's eye and just shook his head slowly as he laughed quietly at his son's youthful candor.

"Your grandmother has a surprise for you," Susannah told Ryan a short time later when they were in their seats, awaiting takeoff.

"She does? What kind of surprise?"

"She wanted to do something special for you, so she planned a party for tomorrow afternoon and invited all your old friends. What do you think about that?"

"Seriously?"

"Seriously, I could hardly believe it myself, but it was her idea. She and Grandfather miss you too," Susannah said softly.

They spent the short flight from Richmond to Philadelphia talking about the days ahead and speculating on the surprise party Ryan's grandmother was planning.

That evening, they got takeout from their favorite pizza place and ate in the living room while they watched an action movie Ryan picked out.

38

Susannah and Ryan arrived at her parent's house shortly after ten the next morning. Frederick was in his study but came out quickly when he heard them come through the front door.

"Hello there, my boy! Come give your grandfather a hug." Ryan ran to Frederick and hugged him tightly. "How was your trip?" he asked his daughter, looking at her over Ryan's head.

"Perfectly uneventful," she replied with a smile as she leaned in to kiss him on the cheek. "Where's Mother? I thought she'd be waiting by the front door," she said lightly, thinking about how excited her mother seemed at the thought of Ryan's visit.

"Taking care of some, ah, last-minute details," he said with a wink. "She'll be along in a moment. In the meantime, I have something to show my grandson, if you can spare him for a few moments."

"Show me what?" Ryan asked, excited by the prospect of a surprise. "Can I go?" he asked Susannah. "Please?"

"Of course you can," she said easily. "I'm going to go see what's keeping your grandmother."

"Where did you get that?" Ryan asked, in awe of the large carved giraffe his grandfather proudly displayed in his library. "Did you go to Africa again?" he asked, slightly disappointed, "Without me?"

"Wouldn't dream of it, my boy," Frederick said jovially. "A promise is a promise. Next time I go, you go. Assuming, it's okay with your dad, that is.

"I already told him," Ryan said candidly, "so he can be thinking about it."

"You remind me so much of your mother," Frederick said, smiling proudly at his grandson. "She was always covering her bases, making sure everything was taken care of. No surprises. Well, until she had you, that is. That was certainly a surprise for us and a welcome one!"

"Did she tell you about my dad?"

"Not at first. She was very sad when they split up and didn't want to talk to us about it. Eventually, with your aunt, Susannah's help, she decided to tell us of her marriage to your dad and that she was expecting a baby. Until then, we never even knew she had gotten married. We just assumed she had broken up with a boyfriend. She was going to college in California then, so we didn't see her very often. Margaret was quite a free spirit."

"Ryan! Come and give your grandmother a big hug," Charlotte said loudly as she entered the library, arms outstretched.

"Hello, Grandmother," Ryan said as he hugged her tightly.

"I swear you've grown another foot since I saw you last," Charlotte exclaimed, stepping back and looking at Ryan proudly. "Are you eating well? Is your dad feeding you? You look thin, Ryan. Are you hungry? Let me make you a sandwich."

"Mother, the party will be starting soon, and the caterers are already setting up. I'm sure he's fine."

"Well, just a snack then," she said as she led Ryan out of the library and steered him toward the kitchen. The last thing Frederick and Susannah heard was "How about some fried chicken? A growing boy has to eat."

"Susannah," Frederick said to his daughter as she turned to leave, "can we have a chat about Ryan?"

"Of course, Father. What's on your mind?"

"It's time to tell him the truth about his mother." "The truth about what exactly?"

"That I am not her biological father. You know I have always treated her as my own," he said quickly when Susannah began to object, "but the truth is I'm not her father. I tried several times over the years to talk with Charlotte about it, to find out more about Maggie's real, father but she wouldn't discuss it. Said it was in her past where it belonged."

"She has always been so secretive about her life before she met you," Susannah agreed, "but Maggie knew. She told me once that she used to ask about her first father. That's how she referred to him, but Mother would never tell her anything. She just said that you were her father now. She finally just stopped asking."

"I received a call from Tom a few days ago. He told me that he knew who Maggie's father was, and that man wanted to tell Ryan. After all, he deserves to have a relationship with his grandson."

"You heard this from Tom?" Susannah said incredulously. "How would Tom know that you aren't Maggie's biological father?"

"Well, Your mother has been to Magnolia Creek before. That's where she and Maggie were from."

"You've got to be kidding," Susannah said in disbelief. "There's more," Frederick said slowly. "He'll soon be living right next door to his biological grandfather."

"How is that possible? Wait, you know who he is?"

"Yes, and so do you. It's Annie's neighbor Arvin Sturgis." "No."

"Yes. Annie sent Ryan and the other kids to take him a plate of Christmas dinner because he refused her invitation to join us. She said he seemed harmless but was a total recluse. When Tom called to talk with me about it, he explained that Arvin's wife had taken their four-year-old daughter Margaret and left him nearly thirty years ago. He was devastated by the loss and hasn't been the same since."

"How on earth did this come to light? Does Ryan know?" she asked quickly, as it dawned on her that he may already know.

"No, he does not know. Tom insisted that we have time to break the news about Maggie's relationship with me before Arvin talks. We need to this weekend. There's no putting it off anymore. It wouldn't be fair to Ryan or to Arvin to deny them that relationship. There has been far too much time lost already with Charlotte and Maggie's decisions to keep their secrets."

"But how did Tom find out?" Susannah asked again. "Frederick, are you coming to join the party? Oh, there you are, Susannah," Charlotte said as she came into the library. "What's keeping you two? The party is about to start."

"We'll be right there, Mother just filling Father in on our trip to Richmond and lunch with Tom."

"Well, don't belong. The guests are beginning to arrive. It's rude to keep them waiting."

"Yes, dear, we're right behind you," Frederick assured his wife.

As Charlotte headed back to the party, Frederick quickly told Susannah the story, Tom had relayed to him about Arvin overhearing Charlotte's voice as they were leaving on Christmas day and then putting the pieces together when he overheard Ryan talking about Maggie. "It seems that Arvin made a tree swing for his daughter all those years ago and frequently visit the site to feel close to her. He even carved her name on the seat of the swing. Ryan saw it and commented on the name being the same as his mother in heaven. When he put it all together, he realized his beloved Margaret was gone, but Ryan was there, practically living next door."

"What are you going to do about Mother?"

"I am going to talk to her tonight and settle this once and for all. How do you feel about being part of the conversation with Ryan? I think it would help him to have you there."

"Of course, anything I can do to help."

"Okay, it's settled then. I'll talk to your mother about it tonight, and we'll tell Ryan tomorrow."

"I'm proud of you, Father," Susannah said as she hugged her father. "You were a great father to Maggie, and you still are to me."

39

"Becca? It's Mary Reed. How are you, Dear?"

"Hello, Mary! What a pleasant surprise. Is everything okay?"

"Everything is great, Becca. We need your help with something, and we'd like to keep it between us until after the wedding. Would you be okay with keeping our secret from Annie and Tom for a couple of months? We don't want to put you on the spot. We know that Annie has so much to deal with at the moment, and we want it to be a surprise."

"Since it's you, of course, I'll do what you ask," Becca told her best friend's mother. "How can I help?"

"Pete and I have decided to move back to Magnolia Creek. We hate being so far away from Annie and her new family. Could you help us find a place to rent while we decide where we want to settle permanently?"

"Oh, Mary, I'd be delighted to help you. Annie is going to be ecstatic!

She misses you so much."

"We're planning to tell her when we get there for the wedding, but we want to pick our timing with all that's happening right now. And we still haven't finalized everything with the business, so I suspect it's going to take a couple of months."

"That's perfect," Becca assured her. "Summer is a great time to find rental properties."

"I'm hoping we can make that decision while we're there for the wedding and then return to Seattle for a short time to wrap things up with the business and move out of our house."

"That is so exciting, Mary. Thanks so much for thinking of me. I'll contact our leasing department first thing in the morning and see what we can get lined up for you. I'll be in touch very soon."

"Was that Annie's mom?" Scott asked when Becca hung up the phone and returned to the sofa where they were enjoying movie night sans kids.

"Yes, can you believe it? They're moving back to Magnolia Creek! She asked me to find them a rental to live in while they decide where they want to settle. Oh, Annie is going to be so happy! I wish I could tell her, But I promised."

"Promised what?"

"Oh, Scott, you can't say anything to Tom or Annie. Mary and Pete want to surprise them when they're here for the wedding next month. She doesn't want to add any stress to Annie right now. Besides, it'll be great news whenever it's delivered."

"Hey, Chad, you got a minute?" TJ asked as Chad joined him on the side porch of the Victorian Café.

"What's up, man?"

"Nothing much, just thought I'd stop by, maybe get something to eat, if it's not too much trouble."

"No trouble at all, TJ. Do you like pot roast?" "What's that?" TJ asked him.

"Its roast beef with potatoes and carrots and gravy," Chad told him, surprised that the younger boy had never had it.

"Well, I guess that will be good then," TJ agreed. "Okay, you wait here, and I'll be back in a couple of minutes."

A few minutes later, Chad appeared with a tray full of food and drinks. He balanced it expertly with one hand while setting food and drinks on the table with the other. When he was done, the table was full, and TJ was already shoving a fresh hot biscuit in his mouth.

"I hadn't taken my lunch break yet, so I thought I'd bring enough food for both of us. That way, if you don't like something, you can try something else. Sound good?"

TJ just nodded since his mouth was full of biscuits, but he did manage a grin.

"How's the pot roast?" Chad asked a few moments later when TJ slowed down to take a drink of milk.

"It's so good!" he replied. "I've never had that before. Mostly my dad makes stuff out of a box. He said that my mom was the cook in the family, but I don't remember."

"I think it's usually like that in families," Chad replied. "At least it has been in my family. I don't remember much about my dad, but as you can tell, Mom's a really good cook."

"You don't have a dad?" TJ asked as he moved on to the homemade macaroni and cheese with the breadcrumbs on top.

"I have one. Everybody has one, but mine wasn't a good one. My mom took me away when I was still pretty young."

"Why did she take you away?"

"Because my dad one was of those guys who hits his kids."

"You mean she took you away from him just because he hit you? Were you bad?"

"No, but even if I was, he was a lot bigger and stronger than me, so he should never have hit me liked he did. She says the last time he hit me he broke my cheekbone. That's when she left him. She was afraid he was going to keep hurting me."

"What happened to him?" TJ asked, resting his fork in the bowl of sweet corn Chad had pushed in his direction. "Your dad, I mean. Was he mad?"

"Yes, he was. But he couldn't do anything about it because he was in jail."

"In jail? Why was he in jail? Did he steal a car or something?" "No, he was in jail because it's against the law to hit your kid." "It is?" TJ said, wide-eyed.

"It sure is. He could have really hurt me, even killed me, if he was mad enough. That's against the law. If he hit another man that hard, he'd go to jail, so of course, he would go to jail for hitting a little kid that hard. And Mom said that he hit her too. But she doesn't like to talk about it much, says that we're just better off without him."

Chad looked directly at TJ for a moment, and when TJ started to shift in his seat, Chad grinned broadly and asked, "Are you ready for dessert? I thought we should try them all. What do you think?"

"I think I'm going to explode!" TJ said, laughing, letting the uncomfortable moment pass.

"Okay, how about you give me a hand with these dishes and we'll grab the dessert tray while we're in there. What do you say?"

"Let's do it!" TJ replied, watching how Chad stacked the plates and cups then holding out his arms to carry them inside.

40

"I invited Arvin Sturgis to the wedding," Annie announced casually to the women sitting in high-backed chairs around the table in the solarium at Magnolia Lane. "After all," she said slowly, as she paused for maximum dramatic effect, "he's family."

When she'd finished her statement, Annie raised her teacup slowly to her lips, watching the women as she sipped her tea, focused primarily on Lillian to gauge her reaction.

While expecting an exclamation of surprise or even confusion on her friend's face, Annie was quite unprepared for what she saw and heard next. "Ah, so that's who she is," said Lillian slowly, a smile forming on her lips as she sat her cup down. As she raised her eyes, she looked in turn at Betty Lou and Winnie, her oldest friends now that Annie's Grandma Abby was gone. The women seated across from her looked bewildered and glanced back and forth between Lillian and Annie, hoping for more information to make sense out of what they just heard.

"You knew?" Annie asked Lillian, clearly surprised at the older woman's reaction.

"I suspected," Lillian replied. "That's different. And to be clear, I only recognized that I knew her years ago. Even I hadn't put the pieces together as to who she was, or rather who she had been.

"She, who I thought we were talking about Arvin Sturgis," exclaimed Winnie, clearly confused.

"And why you said he was family," added Betty Lou. "Do you want to tell them, or should I?" asked Lillian. "Be my guest," replied Annie with amusement. "It sounds to me like you had almost figured it out on your own."

"Do you remember my conversation with Ryan's grandmother, Charlotte Davidson, at Annie's house last Christmas?" she asked her friends as they eagerly awaited her explanation.

"No," said Winnie quickly, glancing back and forth between Betty Lou and Lillian.

"Yes," Betty Lou said slowly as the realization dawned on her that Lillian had given her a look that she didn't understand at the time. It had happened right after Lillian told Charlotte that she looked familiar.

Do you remember her reaction?

"What reaction? What are you talking about?" Winnie pleaded, clearly having missed the entire exchange last Christmas.

Betty Lou turned to her and explained, "Do you remember when we were in the kitchen and I said that Lillian had given me a look but I didn't know why?"

"Yes, you said that Lillian thinks she knows something, but you didn't know what."

"Exactly," replied Betty Lou.

"Exactly," what? Winnie exclaimed. She was still not at all sure what they were talking about, "What did you think you knew?" she asked, turning her gaze on Lillian.

"That Charlotte Davidson is Charlene Sturgis, Arvin's ex-wife."

41

"Thanks again for the party, grandmother," Ryan said the next morning at breakfast. "It was so fun to see all my friends again. And the waterslide was awesome!"

"I'm so happy you enjoyed yourself, Ryan. Your grandfather and I have certainly enjoyed our time with you this weekend. We'll have to make plans to do this as often as possible."

"And you can come and visit me and Dad and Annie anytime too. After they get married, Dad and I are moving into Annie's house, and there's lots of room for you."

"Well, we certainly appreciate that, Ryan. Your grandmother and I look forward to spending more time in Magnolia Creek, don't we, dear?"

"Yes, yes of course," Charlotte said unconvincingly. "Don't you like it there, Grandmother?" Ryan asked, confused by Charlotte's reaction. "Ryan, there's something we need to talk about it. Let's you and I have a man-to-man conversation in the library. How does that sound?"

"Okay," Ryan said as he followed his grandfather into the library and took a seat in one of the leather club chairs in front of the large stone fireplace.

Frederick fixed them both a glass of water on the rocks and handed one to Ryan as he took his seat across from his grandson.

"You've been through a lot of changes in the past couple of years, Ryan, and you have handled it all beautifully. You're becoming a delightful young man, and I'm proud to call you my grandson."

"Thanks, grandfather," Ryan said proudly.

"There is something that you don't know about your mother and her relationship with me. I believe it's time to change that. It's nothing bad, but a man has a right to know who his family is."

Ryan studied his grandfather intently as Frederick searched for the right words.

"Your grandmother was married to someone else when she was very young. Kind of like your mom and Tom." He paused to gauge Ryan's reaction to this news. Not seeing one, he continued. "And much like your situation, your mother was very young when her parents split up. She had very few memories of her real father. She was only four years old when her mother left and took her away from him."

"So you aren't my grandfather?"

"I am your grandfather, Ryan, and I always will be. Don't ever doubt that, okay? Just because I am not your mother's biological father, I still consider her my daughter and you are my grandson. Do you understand?"

"Is Aunt Susannah my real aunt?"

"Yes, she is. She and your mother were half-sisters. That means they both had the same mother, your grandmother Charlotte, but different fathers. I am Susannah's biological father."

Ryan looked a bit confused and sat quietly digesting this news.

"You are our family, Ryan. That will never change. I just thought it was important for you to know you have another grandfather that would like very much to know you and be a part of your life. Your mother never had the chance to know him. Your grandmother decided not to tell her about her past so she would never feel that she wasn't a part of this family. I know you can handle the truth, Ryan, and I don't want your biological grandfather to miss out on having a relationship with you."

"Have you met him? Is he nice?" Ryan asked cautiously. "I have not met him personally, but Annie and your dad have met him and talked with him. They wanted to be sure he was a good man and had good intentions in wanting to get to know you. They will always look out for you, Ryan. They love you as much as we do. If they say it's okay to meet your grandfather, then it's okay. If you want to."

"I think I should think about this. I mean, I want to meet him, but I think I shouldn't rush into it. I mean, I didn't even know about him. My mom never told me either."

"She was so young when she came to live here. As she grew older, she would just have an occasional memory of living someplace else. I'm sure that with her illness, she felt you had enough to deal with."

"But she didn't even tell me about my father," Ryan said, becoming slightly agitated. "Why would she do that? Didn't she know how that felt to not know her father?" He looked pleadingly at Frederick to help him understand. "Maybe I can help with that," Susannah said as she came into the room and sat down beside Ryan and her father. "Excuse me for a moment," Frederick said as he rose from his chair. "I'm going to ask your grandmother to join us so we can all talk about this together and answer any questions you may have."

"Your mother loved your father with her whole heart," she began. "I did not agree with her decision to keep you a secret from him."

"Nor did we," Charlotte said as she and Frederick took their seats across from Ryan. "But it was her decision, and we respected her wishes." "But why would she not want him to know? If she loved him so much, why would she lie to him? And to me?" he asked tearfully.

"It's because she loved him so much that she made the decision she did. She knew that if she told him she was pregnant, he would never have gone along with the divorce. She did not want him to feel trapped in a marriage that they both agreed had happened too suddenly. They were so young, and Tom wanted desperately to become an architect. He had already told his parents that he was dropping out of law school, and his father was furious. He expected Tom to become an attorney and join his father's firm one day."

"Is that why they didn't get along for such a long time?" he asked his aunt, wiping his eyes with the handkerchief his grandfather handed him. "Yes, it is. When I told Tom that you were his son, he was shocked but thrilled! We talked about you and Maggie and him and his father quite a bit before he told you the truth. We all needed to be sure that he was ready to be your dad."

"Did he have to think about it?" Ryan asked hesitantly, afraid of the answer but needing to know.

"Not for a second!" Susannah smiled as she thought about Tom's reaction to the news. "He jumped to his feet and shouted 'Ryan is my son! I'm a dad!' He was so happy he cried," she told Ryan as her eyes started to tear up at the memory of that night at the ball field when she'd changed Tom's life forever.

"I remember when he told me," Ryan said, smiling at the memory. "We were at Annie's house after the big cook-out. He asked if my mom ever talked to me about my dad, and I said all I knew was his name was Tom."

"Well," Frederick said as he rose from his chair, "you have a lot to think about, young man, but I want to encourage you to meet your grandfather.

I don't want to see you lose any more time with your family. Talk about it with your dad. I'm sure he can help you make the right decision."

"Just remember that we love you and we are your family too," Charlotte told her grandson as she hugged him tightly.

42

"You're uncharacteristically quiet today," Lillian said to Winnie as they drove into town to meet Annie and Betty Lou for lunch.

"I still can't get over Charlotte Davidson being Charlene Sturgis," Winnie said to her friend thoughtfully. "What are the odds?"

"Very low, I'd imagine, but she didn't move all that far away," Lillian offered. "Can you imagine her surprise when she found out Tom was living here?" She smiled at the thought.

"Do you think they'll tell Ryan while he's visiting? I think Tom said that he told Arvin he couldn't say anything until his grandparents had a chance to tell him their side of the story."

"That's what I heard too. I suppose he'll find out that Frederick is not Maggie's biological father, but I can't see Charlotte going into detail about being Arvin's wife. I suspect she'll leave that to him."

"Do you know why she left?" Betty Lou asked Annie after they'd placed their lunch order. "No one around here has a clue. From what we can tell, she just up and left him one day and took their daughter with her."

"I can't understand how a man can let go of a child and not even fight to see her," Winnie mused aloud.

"I don't know, Winnie," Annie replied thoughtfully. "I can't imagine not kicking and screaming before someone took my child from me. Unfortunately, we may never know. Charlotte has not been forthcoming about it, and I can't see Arvin opening up to us, can you?"

"The truth is," Lillian interjected judiciously, "it's none of our business, as much as we'd all like to know what happened. The important thing is that the truth is out and Ryan has a lot to deal with."

"This is just the beginning of it," Annie reminded them. "He doesn't know about Arvin yet. He only knows that Frederick is not Maggie's birth father and that he has another grandfather out there somewhere that he's never met."

"Out here, you mean," Winnie piped in. "Practically next door. Or he will be soon enough."

"Has Arvin tried to spend any time with Ryan since he found out?" Lillian wanted to know.

"No, he respected Tom's wishes to allow the Davidsons to tell him their side first. Since no one is going anywhere anytime soon, we agreed to give him a week or two to digest this news before springing more on him. He agreed and has kept his distance from all of us."

"He's grieving too, remember. It wasn't that long ago that he found out that his only child had passed away. There's no longer any hope of reconciling with her and building a relationship," Lillian explained solemnly to the others around the table, "no matter how remote that possibility may have been."

43

"How is he doing?" Kate asked her son as soon as she picked up the phone. She was expecting Tom's call to fill her in after Ryan returned from Philadelphia.

"Annie thinks he's doing well, considering all he's been through. We both feel that having me in his life is a huge benefit right now. Finding out he doesn't know his mother's real family and not knowing his father could have created a real crisis of identity for him."

"Well, this certainly is quite a turn of events," Kate told her son. "Did he talk about it on the way home from the airport?"

"He did. We ended up taking Lillian with us since it was such a nice day. Annie drove on the way back, and I sat in the backseat with Ryan. He told me all about the surprise party first, seeing all his friends and the giant slide Charlotte rented for them, and then he told me about the talk with Frederick."

"It sounds like he was relaying the weekend chronologically, not giving extra weight to any one incident. Is that normal?"

"I don't know. It seemed a bit odd to me that he didn't tell me about his family news first, but he may have been working up to it. Or it wasn't more important to him than the party and seeing his friends."

"Maybe he just needs more time to digest it" Kate offered. "That could be," Tom agreed. "Annie is planning to talk with him about it after we get home. With her background in early childhood development and teaching kids his age, she is the expert in the family."

"How's Ryan taking the news?" Mary asked her daughter. Annie had promised to call them as soon as she could when they got home. Her parents were worried about Ryan receiving more news about his family when he'd been through so much change recently.

"He's doing well as far as I can see," Annie replied. "Most kids his age would be trying to make light of it but be talking about it constantly. Ryan isn't like most kids. Being raised by his aunt and grandparents for most of his life and dealing with his mom's death at such a young age has made him a bit more resilient than most kids who are brought up in a traditional home knowing who their parents are."

"Have you talked with him yet?"

"Not yet. I'm planning on putting him to bed tonight, so if the time is right, I'll talk with him then. If not, I'll talk with him over breakfast tomorrow morning. He's on summer break, and Gina is opening the shop for me tomorrow, so we'll have time to talk."

"Has Tom talked with him about it, yet? How is he doing with all this himself? Quite a shock, I'd imagine."

"Tom isn't pushing him to talk about it, which I think is the right approach. He's planning on having Ryan help him with the garden for a while, allowing him to talk if he wants to. As for Arvin being Maggie's dad, I don't know. Tom hadn't seen Maggie in almost ten years, and even when he did know her, she was rebelling against her family's expectations just as he was. I think it was the reason they connected in the first place. Since he didn't know Frederick until he found out about Ryan, I don't think it's such a big change for him. Well, except for the part about Maggie's biological father being our grouchy, old next-door neighbor," she said with a laugh.

"Speaking of your grouchy neighbor, how is he doing? Is he okay with waiting until you and Tom are ready to let him talk with Ryan?"

"He is," Annie replied, "to a point. He's understandably anxious to tell Ryan about his mother, but so far, he's respected our wishes and even agreed that Ryan needed to hear the news from the Davidsons first."

"I'm glad to hear that he's cooperating. It was encouraging that he came to you and Tom before telling Ryan. I don't think anyone knows Arvin Sturgis, except maybe Charlotte Davidson, but I suspect even he's changed somewhat over the years."

"We are grateful to him for handling it that way. I hate to think of the angst it would have caused Ryan to find out all this from Arvin first."

"Has there been any talk of Charlotte and Frederick coming back for a visit soon? Perhaps she will meet with Arvin then? I'm sure whatever happened between them, she could at least tell him about his daughter."

"I haven't heard anything like that, but I don't suppose they can avoid each other forever. Or for more than another month with the wedding coming up. I suppose he could decline our invitation, but I'm not so sure he will. He seems pretty determined to be part of Ryan's life."

"How do you and Tom feel about that?" Mary asked her daughter delicately.

"We are both looking forward to having a relationship with him, whatever that's going to look like. We'll make the effort to include him and see how he responds and take it from there. I think that's all we can do."

"Just a second, honey," Mary said distractedly as she covered the mouthpiece of her phone. "Sorry, your dad wants me to ask how the old truck is holding up."

As Annie filled in her mother, and by extension her father, on how things were at Blooms, Tom and Ryan headed out to the garden they had planted earlier that month in Eva's backyard.

"Ready to get your hands dirty, son?" Tom asked as he handed Ryan a plastic bucket for the weeds.

"I don't know, Dad," Ryan said hesitantly. "I just changed my clothes and Annie will have dinner ready soon."

"Well, it's a good thing those aren't your only clothes then," Tom replied as he pulled up a muddy weed by the roots and flung it at his son's chest. The splat was almost imperceptible, but the damage was done. He looked at his son and broke into a wide grin. "Welcome home, son."

"Ugh! I can't believe you just did that!" Ryan sputtered, looking down at the muddy spot on his clean T-shirt.

"Well, then, you are going to find this hard to believe," he said as he hit him in the side of the leg with a blast from the hose.

The surprise on Ryan's face was genuine but quickly turned to determination. He was not going to be the only one stripping down in the mudroom before dinner!

"Aah!" Ryan yelled as he dove to the ground and grabbed a clump of mud from the edge of the planting beds. "You're going to pay for that one, Dad."

As Ryan rose to his knees to aim, Tom hit him with a clump of mud, right on his shoulder. "So you want to play dirty, huh?" This last taunt was delivered just before he threw his gob of mud and weeds at his father, catching him on his back as he ducked for cover.

While Tom was trying to regroup, Ryan charged. He landed on top of his dad, and they wrestled for the advantage. As Ryan tried to hold him down with one hand and reach for mud with the other, Tom simply reached up and smeared mud on the side of Ryan's face, laughing so hard he couldn't get up. Ryan, taking advantage of the larger man's weakened state, put two hands full of mud in his dad's hair, massaging it in like shampoo.

"Doesn't that feel good?" Ryan asked, grinning through the mud on his face.

"Hey, Tom! Dad wants to talk…" Annie stopped mid-sentence as she took in the scene in the backyard.

"Dad, he'll have to call you back after dinner. He's kind of in the middle of something messy at the moment. Okay, I'll tell him. Bye."

"Do I even want to know?" Annie asked as she put her phone down and sat on the top step. Daisy was already bounding across the yard toward the melee when Annie called her back.

"You need to ask Dad," Ryan said, pointing an incriminating finger at his father. "He started it!"

"Is that so?" Annie turned her attention to Tom, who was grinning like a kid in a mud puddle. Literally.

"What can I say?" he asked candidly. "I missed my son." As Ryan smiled at his dad, Tom turned the hose on him again, and they picked up where they left off, laughing and having a great time.

"Boys," Annie muttered as she rose to go back inside the kitchen. "Dinner is in thirty minutes, and you'd both better be clean before you come to the table!" Annie announced over her shoulder as she stepped inside, leaving the boys to their harmless but filthy mudslinging.

44

"Becca, what a pleasant surprise!" "Come, have a seat," Eva insisted, showing the young woman to a chair in the sitting area between her room and Lillian's. "I'm afraid Lillian isn't here at the moment. She's having lunch with the girls."

"I know. I was hoping to talk with you alone if that's okay."

"Of course, my dear. I'm happy to help. What can I do for you?" "I'm hoping we can help each other. Have you made any plans for your home after Tom and Ryan move in with Annie?" Becca asked the older woman.

"I've been thinking a lot about that lately. I hate to sell the place, but my granddaughter and her husband think it might be a good time to put it on the market. With all the repairs and upkeep Tom has done, it's never been in better shape."

"They're right. It is in great shape, and it will show very well with all the trees and shrubs in bloom."

"I sense a 'but,'" Eva said with a smile.

"But," Becca said slowly, "I do have a proposition for you."

Eva waited expectantly to hear the reason the younger woman chose to pay her a visit when her roommate was gone.

"I wonder if you would consider renting it for some time to a very reliable couple who would take good care of the place for you."

"I'm listening," Eva encouraged with a tilt of her head. "Just between us, Annie's parents are planning to move back to Magnolia Creek after the wedding. But they don't want Annie and Tom to know yet. They don't want to add anything else to their already crazy summer."

"I'm so very happy to hear that," Eva said sincerely. "I'm sure Annie will love having her family close by. And your secret is safe with me," she added with a conspiratorial wink. "They want to look for a place to buy eventually, but they had hoped to find a place to rent for a while first until they decide where to land permanently. Would you be willing to rent to them, perhaps on a shorter-term lease?"

"Of course, my dear. That would be just fine with me. And let's not worry about a lease unless they require one. I'll charge them the same as Tom is paying, and they can just let me know a month or so before they plan to leave so I can get it on the market."

"Oh, Eva. This is great news! I can't wait to tell them and see if they're interested. I wanted to check with you before even mentioning it to them."

"It's good for me too, my dear. I get to put off selling my home, and I know they will take very good care of it for me. Oh, I'm so glad you stopped by. You've made my day!" she said happily, taking Becca's hand in hers.

"I'll give them a call right now to see what they think of the arrangement," Becca said eagerly as she pulled her phone out of her bag.

"While you do that, I'll make us some tea to celebrate," Eva said as she stood up to give Becca a little privacy and to plug in the electric kettle.

"Hi, Mary! It's Becca. Do you have a few minutes to chat? I found you a place to rent that I think you'll be very happy with."

"That's great news, Becca! Hold on a minute while I get Pete on the other phone."

Mary came back a moment later, and Becca heard a click as Pete picked up the extension.

"Hello, Becca. I hear you have some good news for us," Pete boomed into the phone.

"Well, I hope it is. It sure seems like a good match to me. How would you feel about renting the home that Tom and Ryan are living in now?"

"That would be spectacular!" Mary exclaimed.

"I couldn't agree more," Pete said, "but I thought Tom said that Eva was planning to sell the house over the summer."

"She's been thinking about it, but she's not ready to let it go yet. And the thought of having Annie's parents living there is very appealing to her. She's offered to rent it to your month to month to keep your options open for when you find the right place to buy."

"Well, I think I can speak for both of us when I say 'We accept!'" Pete declared.

"Absolutely!" Mary chimed in. "Oh, Becca, it's perfect!"

"Then I'll let Eva know that it's a deal. I'll send you an e-mail later today with the particulars, and once you let Tom and Annie know, you can work out the move-in details with Tom directly. How does that sound?"

"It sounds like we called the right person for help," Mary said sincerely. "Thank you so much Becca for all your help and for keeping our secret." "Congratulations," Becca told Eva as she poured the tea. "They're thrilled with your offer. I told Mary that I'll send them an e-mail with the details later today, and I'll print a copy for you as well if that's okay." "Perfect," Eva replied happily, relieved to be able to put off the sale of her beloved home.

45

"So how was your trip?" Chad asked Ryan as they sat on the back porch steps.

"It was good," Ryan began hesitantly. "No, it was really good. I just found out something I didn't know about my family."

"Want to talk about it?" Chad offered, leaning back against the railing post on the top step where he sat facing Ryan.

"Nah, we should probably go. TJ might be waiting for us."

"He said he was going to be late, so we have some time to catch up," Chad explained.

"I told him I'd be back today, and he said he'd be there," Ryan reasoned. "Did he say why he was going to be late?"

"Something about a new part-time job, but I'll let him tell you about it himself. Besides, I think you have something you want to tell me."

"It's just that last year I only had my aunt and my grandparents, and now I have more family than I ever dreamed of."

"How so?" Chad asked, encouraging Ryan to continue. "Well, for one thing, I now have three grandpas instead of one!"

"Three? How'd you manage that?"

"My grandfather told me that he isn't my mom's real dad." "Whew, that's a big one," Chad admitted.

"How did that happen without you knowing about it?"

"My grandmother was married to some other guy before she married Grandfather, and she and her other husband had a daughter. She took her how much time he took to get ready.

"Well, it's not going to get any better than this"—he indicated his tux—"so if the limo's here, I'd say we're ready to go."

"Is the back door unlocked for the caterers?" Scott asked his friend as they headed out the front door.

"It is," Tom replied, "but thanks for the reminder."

"I'm your best man, Tom. It's my duty," he said with mock seriousness. "And my pleasure, my friend," he added, patting Tom on his shoulder as he closed the front door behind the groom and his entourage.

Ryan and Drew were already in the limo, pushing all the buttons and opening every compartment. Although Drew had only recently turned six, he and Ryan spent a lot of time together and Drew looked up to his friend like an older brother. Besides, no matter how old you are, boys will be boys and a limo is just cool.

"Dad"—Tom paused just as he was about to climb in the car—"I'm glad you're here." He put out his hand to shake his father's and placed his other hand on the older man's shoulder.

"I wouldn't want to be anywhere else," Harrison Walsh told his son as he shook his hand firmly. "Now climb in and let's get you to the church before the bride arrives. It wouldn't do to start your married life by being late," he chided.

"Duly noted," Tom replied. "Any other bits of fatherly advice you want to share before we go?"

"Just one," Harrison said. "Always put your family first. Trust me, you do not want to look back with regret on missed opportunities."

46

"Oh my," Betty Lou said as they entered the narthex in the front of the church, "this is lovely." There were beautiful flowers in pots on either side of the open front doors with the outside pots connected to those inside the doors by flowered vines draped from one to the other.

"I'm not used to coming in through the front door." Winnie chuckled. "I'm usually in the kitchen." She was not working in the kitchen for this event. She and her friends were guests of honor for Annie and Tom's wedding.

Winnie didn't dress up often, but today she was wearing a light blue linen suit that she had purchased just for this occasion. Lillian had told her earlier that the blue suit made her hazel blue eyes shine even brighter. And she'd meant it. Winnie was beaming.

"Hello, ladies." Harrison Walsh's deep voice resonated through the small foyer. "Who would like to go first?"

"I would," Betty Lou spoke up, taking Harrison's arm as she turned to smile at her friends.

"Surprise, surprise," Winnie said aside to Lillian as she waved at Betty Lou. "I can't say that I blame her," Lillian responded honestly. "He's a handsome man. Truth be told, I miss that since Bill died. It's nice to take the arm of a man. I've always loved that about Tom as well. He's so thoughtful to always offer his arm. Just as I was beginning to think that men didn't do that anymore."

"Frederick and Charlotte are here," Winnie pointed out to Lillian, directing her gaze to the groom's side of the aisle. They were seated behind Tom's family on the inside of the aisle.

"And there's Arvin," Lillian added, nodding toward the man sitting alone at the far end of the pew where his ex-wife and her husband sat, no one making eye contact. "It must be very hard for all of them after so many years," Lillian mused.

"Okay, here he comes back," Winnie said, referring to her escort, Harrison Walsh, only half-hearing what Lillian said. "I'm next." She grinned.

"Of course," Lillian said graciously, still thinking about Arvin.

"May I have the honor of escorting you, Miss Lillian?" a familiar voice asked.

She turned slightly to the touch on her arm and found herself looking at Tom.

"What on earth are you doing ushering? You're the groom!"

"I know, but it's my wedding, so I get a little leeway when it comes to protocol. May I?" he asked again, extending his arm to Lillian.

The older woman could not conceal her delight at the special treatment. She and Tom walked slowly and steadily down the aisle of the church past all the pews with beautiful sprays of flowers and ribbons adorning them, stopping at the front row on the left, the one reserved for the bride's family. As she realized where he was seating her and opened her mouth to question him about it, she saw him smile and point to her friends, already seated in the family pew.

She turned to him and, with her free hand steadying his face, kissed him softly on the cheek. He accepted it gracefully and helped her to her seat.

"What?" she said innocently as her friends looked at her with raised eyebrows, "he's allowed." At that moment, Pete arrived to seat his wife next to Lillian. He then returned to the narthex to await his daughter.

"He's so proud," Mary whispered to Lillian, "and I'm so nervous. I just want everything to go perfectly for Annie's special day."

"You have no reason to worry," Lillian told her with a reassuring pat on her knee. "He's here, she's here, and Pastor Bob is here. What could go wrong?"

"What could go wrong?" Scott whispered to Tom with alarm. "Some crazy ex-boyfriend bursts through the doors yelling 'I object!' is what could go wrong, my friend."

As Tom turned to look at his best man, Scott added with a grin, "But if that doesn't happen, you're golden."

"You certainly have a way of putting things into perspective, Scott," Tom whispered, visibly relaxing.

"You look beautiful," Pete said to his daughter as he stood beside her, waiting for their cue to head into the sanctuary. "Thanks, Dad," Annie said calmly. "I expected to be nervous, but I'm not. Is that weird?"

"You're asking the wrong guy, sweetheart," he said with a smile. "But I have to say, weird or not, I think it's a good sign, don't you?"

"I do," she stated emphatically and then laughed. "Just practicing," she said lightly as she smoothed her dress and stood up straight, just as the music started.

"You're going to do great," Pete said as she took his arm. "I could not be a prouder father than I am at this very moment."

"Don't you dare," Annie said under her breath as she noticed the moisture in her father's eyes. "If you do, I will, and I'm not going to cry. Understood?"

"Got it," Pete said with an emphatic nod. He turned his head to the side as he cleared his throat, taking the opportunity to quickly wipe the moisture from his eyes before turning back to his daughter. "All under control."

"Okay then," she said taking a deep breath, "they're playing our song.

Let's do this!"

Harrison Walsh seated his wife in the family pew next to Tom's younger sister Elizabeth. The music began just as he was taking his seat for the ceremony.

Tom caught his eye, and his father gave him a reassuring wink.

The doors opened a moment later, and the bridal party entered the church. As the most beautiful woman in the world made her way slowly toward him, Tom's eyes locked with Annie's. The rest was a bit of a blur.

47

As they stood inside Tom's kitchen, prepared to head into the backyard to meet their guests, Tom turned to his new bride and said, "Ready, Mrs. Walsh?"

"Ready," Annie replied, taking his arm.

"Please welcome Mr. and Mrs. Tom Walsh!" the lead singer of the band announced as they made their entrance. The band started right in on their music set as Tom and Annie made the rounds, speaking to all their guests. Before they took their seats at the head table, they took a few moments to wander around the yard on their own.

"This looks beautiful, Tom. You guys did an amazing job. I'll hate to see the tent come down. It's magical!"

"Well then, it's a good thing, you won't be here to see it. We'll be on our way to New Hampshire while that is happening. Bobby is driving us into the city tonight, and we fly to Boston late tomorrow morning. From there, it's a couple of hours' drive through the scenic countryside to Meredith, New Hampshire, and our beautiful accommodations at the inn on Lake Winnipesaukee. Did I just sound like a game show announcer?" he asked his wife. "I think I did."

Annie just laughed at her husband and said, "You did, and I loved it. I do feel like I just won the bonus prize."

"You must be the Walsh's," Frederick said by way of introduction. "I'm Frederick Davidson, and this is my wife, Charlotte. We're Ryan's grandparents, on his mother's side," he clarified.

"Please, call me Harrison, and this is my wife, Kate. It's a pleasure to meet you. We were hoping to introduce ourselves before the wedding, but as you can imagine, it was a bit hectic."

"Pete and I wanted to express our gratitude to you, ladies, for all you've done for our daughter," Mary began as she and Pete took their seats across from the women who had been such good friends to her mother and now to her daughter. Lillian spoke first. "It has been our pleasure, Mary, I assure you. We were bereft when Abby passed. Her passing left a hole in our hearts and our little group. Annie was a ray of sunshine that Abby sent us to keep us whole. She has been a blessing to each of us as much as we have tried to be for her."

"She looked so much like her grandmother in that dress," Betty Lou said to Lillian as they watched the newlyweds make their rounds to talk to the guests.

"It's hard to believe that Abby has been gone for over a year. I still miss her," Lillian said with a touch of sadness in her voice.

"I do too," Betty Lou agreed, "but you have to admit, she gave us a heck of a substitute!"

"She did at that." Lillian smiled.

"He has every reason to be proud," Harrison said to Kate as he watched Chad taking his mother around to show her all the work they had done to get ready for the reception.

"Is that the young man who was involved in the break-in last year?" Kate asked her husband.

He nodded. "Hard to believe, isn't it?"

"I don't know how we managed it, but we certainly did something right in raising our son. The role model he has become to Chad and Ryan makes me so proud."

"And don't forget the baseball team," he added. "I'm sorry to say he didn't learn to catch a ball from me."

"Well, it's never too late," she said brightly, "although you may want to pick something other than baseball to teach your son. And then there's Ryan," she added, "he'd love to play catch with his grandfather. I think he'd love to do just about anything with you."

As if on cue, Ryan came running up to Harrison and Kate, slightly out of breath and smiling. "Grandpa, can you help me? I'm trying to—"

"Do you mind?" Harrison asked his wife as he handed her his champagne glass.

"Not at all," she said. "Go and have fun with your grandson!" "Chad, you boys did a great job in getting the house ready for the reception," Kate said as the young man made his way over to her to say hello. "Thanks, Mrs. Walsh, but it was nothing. Just helping out a little when Tom needed me."

"Your mother tells me that you're planning to stay at Annie's house and take care of Daisy while they're away for their honeymoon," she continued as Chad took Harrison's recently vacated seat.

"Now that I have a car, it'll be easy to get back and forth to work, and it'll be best for Daisy to be in her own house.

She's moved around a couple of times since Annie's grandma died. Besides," he added, "I can take care of watering the flowers and keep an eye on things while they're gone."

"I know Tom is happy to have someone he trusts taking care of the place for him. He speaks very highly of you," she added. "Did you know that?"

"I didn't know he talked about me at all," he said with a smile, clearly pleased to know Tom told his mother about him.

"Oh yes," Kate continued, "he says you're a remarkable young man and he's lucky to know you. He also said you're a whiz on the computer and you also help out your mom at the café."

"Well, I'm pretty good with the computer, but most older people think I'm super good because they don't always understand it all. Our generation just makes it look easy since we grew up with computers."

"Well, Tom's not prone to exaggeration, so I'm going to believe that you're a whiz if that's okay with you." She smiled warmly.

"Don't leave," Charlotte said to her husband as they watched Arvin make his way over to them.

"You need to clear the air with him," Frederick said softly to his wife, squeezing her hand as he did so. "I'll be close by, and I promise to keep an eye on you and intervene if you need me."

"Arvin," Frederick said, reaching out to shake the other man's hand. "I'll give you two some time to talk," he said as he released Arvin's hand and moved away.

"Thanks," Arvin said softly, not noticing that Frederick had already stepped away. His gaze was completely focused on Charlotte.

"He seems nice," he began, referring to Frederick.

"He is a very nice man," Charlotte began, a bit defensively. "And he is not the reason—"

"You look good, Charlie," Arvin continued, not listening to Charlotte's defense of her husband.

"No one has called me that for over thirty years," she said softly. "I just wanted to say I'm sorry."

"Why are you sorry? I'm the one who left."

"I'm sorry you felt that was your only way out. I'm sorry that I didn't come after you. I'm sorry that I never saw my daughter again, and I'm sorry that now I never will," he said hurriedly as if he needed to get it all out in one breath. He hadn't said that many words at one time in his entire life.

"I'm sorry too, Arvin. I know that I should never have taken your daughter away from you. I was angry, and I felt trapped here. But it doesn't matter now, does it?"

"Are you happy?" he asked. "I am."

"Ryan is great. You must have done a good job raising our Maggie." "She had a good life, Arvin. She was happy and loved, and she was taken from all of us way too soon."

"Okay then" was all he said. He turned and walked away without another word, but he didn't leave the party. Instead, he went to find Ryan.

"How did it go?" Frederick asked his wife as he handed her a fresh glass of wine.

"He called me Charlie" was all she said. "You okay?"

"I'm good," she said sincerely as she seemed to recover from her thoughts. "It's over, and I'm good."

"Well, that's done then," Lillian said quietly as she observed the exchange from a distance. "Now they can all move on."

48

"Annie, you're back! How was your trip? How's Tom? How's Ryan? Did he enjoy camp this year?"

"It was great, Mom. Everyone had a great time, but we are all so glad to be home. Tom and Ryan are over at their place packing the last of their things."

"Honey, I'm so glad you're back," Mary said.

"We both are," Pete said as he picked up the extension. "We can't wait to hear all about your trip."

"That sounds great," Annie replied. "Tom and I were talking, and we feel bad that you have been here several times since I moved here but we haven't been out to see you. What do you think about us coming out next month for a visit before Ryan starts school?"

"You mean come to Seattle?" Mary asked, stalling for time to think. "Sure, you make the trip all the time, we feel like it's our turn to come to you!"

"Well, that's thoughtful of you, sweetheart, but I don't think that's going to work out," Pete told his daughter. "Really?" Annie asked, confused by her dad's reaction.

"Why not?"

"Because we'll be in Magnolia Creek in a couple of weeks, dear," Mary explained.

"I don't understand. You're coming back so soon? Not that I mind at all, I'm just surprised," Annie explained.

"I know, dear. We didn't want to tell you until after the wedding."

"What do you mean? Tell me what?"

"Your father and I decided we are entirely too far away from our favorite people in the world, so we're moving back to Magnolia Creek."

"Seriously? You're moving here? When? Oh my gosh! Wait until I tell Tom and Ryan! They'll be thrilled!"

"We were hoping to tell you all together, but with your news about a visit out here, we thought it best to tell you now."

"I'm so excited! When will you be getting here? What will you do with all your things? You'll be staying with us, of course. I'll make sure your room is ready, and I can set up the extra guest room as a den for you so you have somewhere to get away from the chaos that is our life," she added happily.

"Slow down, honey. We're not staying with you," Pete interjected. "We know we're welcome, but you have your own family now, and we want to be close to you all, not on top of you."

"Where are you going to live then?"

"Well, as soon as your new husband and son vacate the premises, we'll be moving into Eva's house," Pete said.

"So that's why she was so secretive about what she was doing with the place. Tom wondered why she wasn't asking for his help to get it on the market or talk to new tenants. I told him it was probably because she didn't want to burden him with all the wedding planning going on."

"Well, that and we asked them not to tell you," Mary added. "Them?" Annie asked her mother. "Whom exactly did you tell?" "Well, we started with Becca, and she talked to Eva. I'm sure she told Scott, but they kept our secret because we asked them to."

"I see," Annie said thoughtfully. "Our best friends kept a secret from us for how long?"

"Just a couple of months," Mary said quickly. "It was important to us that you not have one more thing to think about while you planned for your wedding."

"But they would know that this is great news, and they still kept it a secret."

"They were doing their jobs," Pete said. "After all, they were your best man and matron of honor, right? It was their job to keep you two as focused and stress-free as possible. I'd say they did a brilliant job, wouldn't you?"

"I have to admit they did do a great job. I'm quite sure we didn't make it easy for them," she added.

49

"Thank you for meeting with us, Eva. This is such a lovely spot," Mary told the older woman as she and Pete sat down at the table on the verandah of Magnolia Lane. "We just wanted to stop by and thank you again for allowing us to stay in your lovely home."

"It is a nice place," Pete added politely. "Very well maintained," "You have your son-in-law to thank for that." Eva smiled. "Tom was such a godsend to me. I never wanted to sell the old place, but it needed quite a bit of work that Tom assured me he was looking forward to doing." "From what he's told us," Mary told her, "he loved every minute of it." "So how was the move?" Eva asked as they enjoyed their lemonade under the large circulating paddle fans on the screened porch. "Uneventful," Pete declared. "Just the way I like it."

"Our car was delivered a few days after we arrived, and the furniture we don't need right away is now safely stored in your garage."

"That sounds like a good move to me." Eva smiled, pleased with the way the entire situation had worked out.

"What a pleasant surprise," Lillian said as she arrived at the table to join her roommate for a light lunch.

"Lillian," Pete said in greeting as he stood and pulled out her chair, "it's nice to see you again." He gave her a peck on the cheek as Mary came around to give her a proper hug.

"I didn't know you'd be joining us," Lillian said to her friend. "This is a nice surprise."

"Pete and I just stopped by to thank Eva for allowing us to stay in her lovely home. It's just perfect for us."

"You must join us for lunch," Eva insisted. "The food here is wonderful, and you'll be our guests."

"We would love to, thank you," Mary said after a quick look at her husband.

"Annie tells me that you've reconnected with some of your old friends," Lillian began while they ate their lunch. "How is that going for you?"

"In some cases, it's like we never left," Mary said.

"In others, it's like we never knew each other," Pete added. "Funny how that happens."

"I know you haven't been back very long," Eva asked conversationally, "but have you found enough to keep you busy?"

"Oddly, we have," Mary responded. "We often wonder how we ever got anything done when we were both working. We just seem to have lots to do all the time."

"I know this whole retirement thing is new for you, Pete," Lillian said. "From what I hear, keeping busy is the key. Would you agree?"

"Since it's still summer break for Ryan, we've been able to spend a lot of time with him. He's very interested in learning how to use tools to help his dad fix things around the house."

"I've been teaching him to play a little piano," Mary added. "His mother taught him some basics when he was younger. When she got sick, they stopped playing. He says it reminds him of her, so I'm teaching him a few songs rather than traditional lessons, at least for now."

50

"There it is," Ryan announced as he and his grandpa Reed pushed through the last of the brush that gave way to the clearing around the old house.

"I don't think I ever knew this place was here," Pete said in wonder at the old farmhouse that stood in front of him. "She's a beauty."

"Wait 'til you see what TJ, I, and Chad have done to fix it up," Ryan said enthusiastically.

"TJ, Chad, and I," Pete said absently, his mind taking in the homestead in front of him, the possibilities swirling in his brain.

"Chad and you?" Ryan asked Pete, not registering what his grandpa meant or why he was so fascinated by the old house. After all, he hadn't even shown him the best parts yet.

"What?" Pete asked, focusing on Ryan again. "Never mind, let's see what you boys have been up to," he continued, heading toward the front porch.

"Grandpa Arvin helped us fix the front porch steps so no one would get hurt, but the rest of the work was all TJ, me, and Chad."

"Well, that was smart," Pete said as he went up the new steps to the old wrap-around porch. Your grandpa has lived here all his life. Does he know who owns this old place?"

"He does," Ryan said. "It's where he and Grandma Charlotte lived with my mom when she was a little girl. He even made a swing for her over there," he said, pointing vaguely in the direction of the old tree.

"Is that so?"

"Yep, He told me that as long as we were careful we could use it as a clubhouse. We just can't go near the barn, and we have to let him know if any of the floorboards are loose so he can help us fix them. Pretty cool, right?"

"I'd say so!" Pete replied. "Let's go see what you've done with this new clubhouse of yours."

Ryan held the screen door open as he opened the front door, standing back to let his grandpa go in first. Pete noticed the huge grin on his face and could feel Ryan's pride at sharing his special place with his grandpa.

"This is the living room," Ryan said with a sweep of his hand. "We pretty much just use this for resting after a hard day of work on the place," Ryan explained. Pete grinned at his grandson as he continued the tour. As he followed Ryan to the back of the house toward the kitchen, Pete took in the furniture and fixtures that remained. It was as if the family had just walked away from the house many years ago.

The kitchen they walked into was quite large and still had the old farmhouse sink. Some of the windows were broken, but many had survived the years of neglect. The old fridge was still there, but the handle and lock had been removed. It looked like it hadn't worked in many years, but it was clear by the marks on the door that the safety precaution was new.

As they ascended the stairs, Pete was impressed with how solidly the house had been built. The handrail didn't budge, and only a few of the stair treads creaked under his weight.

There were four bedrooms upstairs and a large bath at the end of the hall. There was evidence of rodents and some damage to the furniture that had been left behind. The humid Virginia summers had taken their toll on the more delicate pieces.

As they headed back downstairs, they heard TJ approaching, calling to Daisy as he bounded up the front steps.

"Hey, girl where's Ryan?" he asked her as he rubbed her head and ears.

"Oh, hi, Grandpa Reed," TJ said as he saw Pete and Ryan heading toward the open front door.

"Hi, TJ, Ryan is giving me the tour. Nice place you have here."

"We were just going to the cellar to check out our workshop," Ryan said as he smiled at his friend. "Grandpa is a plumber and knows a lot about fixing things," Ryan added as he led the group to the cellar door off the kitchen.

There was no electricity running in the old house, but once his eyes adjusted to the dim lighting, Pete was able to see quite well in the cool, damp space.

"There wasn't a lot of light down here, so we got creative," TJ told the older man. "We cleaned all the windows, and Grandpa cut back the weeds and bushes that were blocking the light."

"Then we found some mirrors and shiny platters and cleaned them up too," Ryan added. "When we put them near the windows, we got a lot lighter."

"Well done, boys," Pete said sincerely. "You've done an incredible job. I'm impressed."

The boys beamed at each other, clearly happy with the high praise from Pete.

"So what are you working on here?" Pete asked as he looked at the worktable they made from two sawhorses covered with several boards and about a half a sheet of plywood. "We wanted to build a tree house, but we haven't got enough wood. Next time Grandpa Arvin comes over, we're going to ask him if he can go into the barn with us to find some more. He said it's too dangerous to go in there without him since its falling."

"Good call. You never know if even one step could send it all tumbling down. Better to let someone who knows the place decide if it's safe. Sounds like your Grandpa Arvin is watching out for you."

"Let's show him the hammocks!" TJ said, suddenly remembering they had not finished the tour. "You're going to love those, Grandpa Reed!" TJ said enthusiastically. He had taken to calling Pete Grandpa Reed from the first time they'd met. Pete couldn't be happier.

51

"Are you feeling okay, Annie? You look a little pale this morning."

"I'm okay, Gina. Just dragging a little these day, I thought that after the wedding was over, things would settle down a bit. I was wrong," Annie said wearily.

"Settle down? Where? Business is great, and you have a new husband and son in your house full time now."

"True," Annie conceded, "but with all the scheduling and decisions that had to be made for the wedding, I thought normal life would be a little less hectic."

"Have you given Ryan chores to do? You know boys his age have unlimited energy that needs to be directed. You'd be doing him and you a favor by teaching him life skills. Like doing dishes, taking out the trash, cleaning his room, feeding the dog, you know, life skills," Gina said with a smile.

"I didn't need to. Ryan is a great help around the house, as is Tom. They had it all worked out ahead of time as to what their chores were going to be and how they can help me and not add to my already crazy schedule. From taking care of Daisy to cleaning the floors, they have it covered."

"So what's the problem?"

"Truthfully, I don't know. As far as I can tell, I don't have any trouble sleeping. Tom hasn't noticed me waking up in the middle of the night, and he's a fairly light sleeper. I just feel tired when I get up, and today my stomach was a little upset. Fortunately, Tom and Ryan are used to being self-sufficient for breakfast, so I don't have to worry about fixing them anything."

"Well, that works out great for you then, doesn't it?" Gina asked, knowing Annie didn't usually eat first thing in the morning.

"It does," Annie replied, "especially lately. I just haven't had much of an appetite. I'm sure it's nothing to worry about," Annie continued, "and it's a good thing for my waistline. I'm not used to eating big dinners, but with a man and a growing boy in the house, we cook almost every night."

"Happy?" Gina asked.

"Very" Annie replied with a contented smile. "Life is good."
"Excellent! Well, those flowers are not going to arrange themselves,"
Gina said as she stood and stretched. "I'll let you look through the orders while I start pulling the stock out of the big cooler."

Less than an hour later, the shop was open for business, and then displays the two women had created that morning were sitting in their vases and pots, just waiting to brighten someone's day.

It wouldn't take long for them to sell. Blooms had done a healthy amount of business in the area since it opened last summer. Several local artists displayed their wares among the flowers and plants placed strategically throughout the room, creating an ambiance of creativity and serenity. The shop's location on the historic town square was the perfect spot to generate a steady stream of foot traffic from both locals and visitors. Magnolia Creek was a quaint town with a rich history and all the modern conveniences of more crowded urban areas. Many of the town's more recent inhabitants chose to relocate to the area to enjoy a break from the traffic and crowds of the larger cities like Richmond to the east, Lynchburg to the west, and Charlottesville to the north.

"Feeling better?" Gina asked, noting that Annie looked refreshed and had not had any trouble keeping up the pace needed to get their orders filled and the shop displays restocked.

"I am," Annie replied. "I think it's the flowers. There's just something about them that makes me happy."

52

"I'm going to Grandpa's house, Mom. I'll be back before supper!" Ryan's feet barely touched the floor as he came flying down the stairs, turning the corner into the kitchen, and grabbing his jacket from the hook by the back door.

Annie stood at the kitchen sink looking out over the backyard, admiring what was left of the changing leaves. It was barely eight o'clock on Saturday morning, and she was enjoying her first cup of coffee as she heard Ryan's footsteps and turned to greet him.

"Wait a sec," she said quickly, trying to catch Ryan before he was through the back door. At the speed he was moving, he'd be across the backyard before she finished her sentence.

"What's the rush? How about a 'good morning, Mom' or maybe 'you look beautiful this morning, Mom'?"

Annie smiled at her son as he wheeled around, shrugging into his jacket as he reached for the door handle.

"He said I could drive the tractor today," Ryan exclaimed with a huge grin, sure that was all the explanation Annie needed.

"That's great, Ryan," Annie said, smiling appreciatively. "No wonder you're excited. I'm really happy you enjoy spending so much time with your granddad, but we have rules and you have chores. Did you—" Annie began before being cut off by her son as he shifted impatiently from one foot to the other, anxious to be on his way.

"Yes," Ryan said quickly, anticipating her questions. "I fed Daisy, gave her fresh water, made my bed, put my pajamas in the hamper, and brushed my teeth."

"Well, I'm impressed," Annie said truthfully. "It seems like there's just one more thing to do then."

"What?" Ryan asked, furrowing his brows as he tried to think of what he missed. He couldn't think of a thing. When he looked up, Annie was smiling at him, tapping her cheek with her finger.

Ryan grinned, gave Annie a quick kiss on the cheek, and headed for the door. "Thanks, Mom!" he yelled over his shoulder as he sailed off the back porch, feet never touching the steps.

"Have fun and do as your granddad tells you," she said loudly as she watched Ryan disappear into the trees that separated her property from the Sturgis farm.

"Where's he off to in such a hurry?" Tom asked his wife as he came into the kitchen carrying a large, dusty old box. "Grandpa's letting him drive the tractor today!" she said with a smile, mimicking Ryan's enthusiasm.

Tom laughed with her as he continued to make his way across the kitchen toward the door.

"Tom?" Annie asked, shifting her full attention to her husband. "Why are you carrying that dusty, dirty box through my nice clean kitchen?"

"Uh," Tom stalled, looking at the floor where the dirt was falling and then quickly stealing a glance at the back door, clearly gauging the distance to make a hasty exit.

"Good morning, Mary!" Tom called out, seeing his mother-in-law step onto the back porch. "Come on in."

"You girls have a nice time today. I'll be in the barn if you need me," he said as he made a hasty departure without even a backward glance at his wife.

"Did I interrupt something?" Mary asked with amusement as she hung her jacket on a hook by the backdoor.

"Not really," Annie replied. "Ryan just flew out of here to go to Arvin's house, and Tom was trying to get out of explaining why he was carrying an incredibly dirty box across my clean kitchen."

"What's he working on out there?" Mary asked as she took a seat at the kitchen table while Annie poured her coffee. "Something for Ryan's room. I think he's making him a desk or table where he can use the computer and do his homework."

"It sure is handy to have someone around who knows how to design things as well as build them!"

"He loves building things, especially furniture. I think he has a real gift for it."

"Well, I'm sure having an old house to keep up and a new family to build for is just what he needs." Mary smiled as Annie sat down with her second cup of coffee.

"I can't believe it's the last weekend of the farmer's market. This year has certainly flown by!" Annie exclaimed as she and her mother prepared their shopping lists.

"I see you are planning to get a bushel of apples," Annie noticed. "You don't need to buy apples, Mom. We told you that you're welcome to all the apples you want from the orchard."

"Aren't you planning to make applesauce this year?" Mary asked her daughter.

"It sounded like a great idea this summer," Annie admitted, "but I just don't have the energy. The guys will eat a lot of them, but we have way more than we need. You'd be doing us a favor by taking them off our hands," Annie insisted. "I'll have Tom take you into the root cellar near the barn where we store them to keep them fresh. Just tell him how many bushels you want, and he'll set them aside for you. He and Ryan can bring them over to you whenever you're ready," Annie assured her mother. Take as many as you can use. We plan to give the rest to the food bank over the next several months."

"Well, then I happily accept," Mary told her daughter. "I've loved those apples since I was a little girl. If there's enough, I can always keep some to make pies with for the holidays."

"Trust me," Annie replied, "there are enough!"

"Then I'll make applesauce for your family as well!" Mary decided. "What else can I do for you, honey? I'm happy to help out whenever you need me," Mary said eagerly.

"Thanks, Mom, but I can't think of anything in particular right now." "You know, it's not healthy for your father and me to spend all our time together," she said with a laugh. "I've spent so much time making sure that he stays busy that I haven't spent much time figuring out what I want to do now that I'm retired too."

"You just stop by here or the shop anytime you feel like you need a break. I'm sure I can find something to keep you occupied."

"I hope you mean that, Annie. I just might take you upon it. I would love to be useful. You know after I get tired of sleeping in every day!"

"Ugh," Annie groaned. "Those days are over for me for a while. With a family and a business, there just aren't enough hours in the day."

"Then by all means let me help," Mary urged her daughter. "When can you start?" Annie asked with a laugh as she stood up to get more coffee. She'd already had two cups, she realized, and it wasn't yet nine o'clock in the morning. The way she'd been feeling the last few days, she might need a fourth just to keep going.

"How about right now?" Mary said as Annie sat back down beside her at the table. "Seems to me you could use a few more hours of sleep. Why not let Dad and I get what you need from the farmers' market. He should be back from the barber in a little while, and I'm sure he won't mind. He enjoys all the free samples."

"Oh, I can't ask you to do that. I'm sure I'll be fine when I get moving."

"You didn't ask," Mary reminded her. "I offered. As much as I enjoy spending time with you, it seems to me that you have a rare opportunity with both Tom and Ryan out of the house. Take it, sweetie," she encouraged her daughter.

"That sounds incredibly tempting, but I can't."

"You can. Now listen to your mother and go back to bed." When Pete and Mary returned from the market a couple of hours later, Mary was surprised to find that her daughter was still sleeping. She peeked in on her, as any mother would, and found her sleeping soundly. One of the bedroom windows was open, letting in a cool breeze along with the warm dappled sunlight that was coming through the trees.

The old-fashioned bell sounded as a woman entered the flower shop through the front door.

"Good morning, sunshine!" she said loudly. "My, aren't you just glowing?"

"Winnie! What a nice surprise. What brings you in here today?" Annie asked her friend as she gave the older woman a welcoming hug.

"I was hoping you could help me surprise Lillian. Betty Lou and I want to throw her a party for her birthday in a couple of weeks. She'll be eighty-five, and we think it's worth celebrating."

"It sounds wonderful. How can I help?"

"We'd like to have the party at Magnolia Lane so all her friends there can attend. I spoke to the woman in charge of events, and she said it would be best to have it during the week since many people visit their families on the weekend. Since her birthday isn't until Sunday, we thought we'd have a chance of actually surprising her with a party midweek. What do you think?"

"I think she's lucky to have such thoughtful friends," Annie replied. "We're planning it for Wednesday morning, two weeks from today.

Can you make something special for her? You know how much she loves your flowers, Annie."

"Of course, and I have just the thing in mind," Annie said, grabbing her pencil and notebook. She began to sketch the flower garden she had in mind, a miniature white picket fence across the back of the long rectangular pot, reminiscent of a garden gate.

"I'll put a variety of flowers in it so they will continue to bloom for several weeks. And I'll have one of our local artists create a sign to hang on the fence with Lillian's name on it. You know, to make it more personal. And when I'm there on Saturdays, I can keep an eye on it and change out the plants as needed."

"That sounds wonderful, Annie. I knew you would come up with the perfect gift. Now I'm off to see Marie at the café to see if she has any ideas for a light brunch. We're planning to have the party right after Lillian's midmorning book club meeting. That way she will be busy while we get everything set up. She'll never expect it on a Wednesday morning the week before her birthday!" Winnie said excitedly. "This time we might just pull off the surprise."

"This time?" Annie asked.

"Well, the truth is we haven't been able to surprise her in years."

"So I take it you and Betty Lou are feeling the pressure to get this one right?" Annie asked sympathetically.

"Yes, several years back, we stopped trying and started going out to dinner. I think we just might be able to pull it off this year. To keep her from suspecting anything, we already made plans to take her to dinner at the new seafood place on Route 15 Sunday after church. You all are welcome to join us. I've been so focused on the party I hadn't even thought to invite you to dinner!"

"That sounds nice, Winnie. I'll talk to Tom about it when I get home tonight, and I'll let you know. You can count on me for the party at Magnolia Lane. Although Ryan will be in school, I'm sure Tom will be there if he can."

"Then we'll just have to save Ryan a big piece of cake.

See you later!" Winnie said over her shoulder as she hurried out to go talk with Marie.

54

"Pete," Arvin said as he shook the other man's hand. "Thanks for meeting me, Arvin," Pete said as he motioned to their waitress.

"Why did you want me to meet you here?" he asked, looking around the small diner.

"Coffee?" the waitress asked Arvin, arriving with pot in hand. "Black, thanks," Arvin said automatically.

When she walked away, Pete got right to the point. "It's about your old house, the one on Smith Lane, out behind my daughter's property."

"What about it?" Arvin asked, sipping his coffee, watching Pete warily. "Ryan showed me around the place a while back. Says you let him and his friend TJ use it as a clubhouse. Nice place."

Arvin's eyes narrowed at Pete's last statement. "Nice place? That house has been abandoned for twenty-five years. I told the boys they could play there as long as they stay away from that old barn. It's not safe. Did he tell you that? Did he tell you that I fixed it up a bit so they wouldn't get hurt?"

"He did," Pete assured the other man, sensing that he was getting defensive. "I think it's great what you've done for them. For him."

"Well, he is my grandson," Arvin said, taking another sip of his coffee, still eyeing Pete, waiting for an explanation of why the man wanted to meet. "Would you consider selling the place?" Pete asked directly. "To me and Mary?"

"Why?" Arvin asked, clearly taken aback by Pete's question. "To live in. It's no secret that Mary and I moved back to Magnolia Creek to be closer to our daughter and her family. We're only renting until we find the right place."

Arvin just listened, trying to come to terms with the idea of someone else living in that house after all this time. "The thing is," Pete continued, "Mary has been trying to get me to retire for over a year. I don't like the idea of retiring, not one bit," he added emphatically, "but I am glad that I decided to get out of the business end of running a plumbing company in Seattle. I like working with my hands, seeing the result of my work at the end of the day."

Arvin continued to watch Pete, listening without saying a word. "Annie is our only child. She's happy here with Tom and Ryan, and we want to be closer to her. I'm sure you can understand that."

"So what exactly are you proposing?" Arvin asked pointedly, sitting back in the booth as the waitress refilled his cup without waiting for him to ask.

"I'd like to restore the house, clean up the yard, and possibly build a new barn that we can use for a garage and workshop. Tom is an amazing carpenter, and I think it would be good for Ryan to be involved in helping us so he can learn some useful skills. Nothing against Frederick, but he wasn't able to teach him how to build or fix anything."

"That's for sure," Arvin said. "She wanted a fancy man and a fancy house, and that's what she got," he added a bit snidely.

"There's a lot that you and Tom and I can teach him, Arvin," Pete said, trying to get keep the other man focused on the conversation at hand. "So what do you say, will you think about it?"

"The property isn't for sale, Pete," Arvin told him.

"I have to tell you I'm disappointed. Mary and I thought this would be a win for all of us, including you," Pete told him.

"Tell Mary I'm sorry but..." he trailed off, not making eye contact with Pete. "I have to go," he said quickly as he stood up and dropped a couple of singles on the table for the coffee.

55

"What can I do?" Tom asked as he came through the back door of the shop, meeting Annie in the hallway next to the office. "The truck is gassed up, washed, and ready to go."

Her grandpa Ben's old truck had been a godsend to her and a major component of keeping her business running. It was the only vehicle she had when she first moved to Magnolia Creek. A couple of months before the wedding, it had broken down while she was on a delivery. She hated to put too much wear and tear on her grandpa's old truck. It was an icon for her business and a special part of her grandpa that she treasured.

While it was being repaired, she and Tom shopped for a more reliable vehicle for her everyday use. They chose an SUV that allowed her the flexibility to carry deliveries should she need to. Annie had been driving the SUV all summer, enjoying the air conditioning her beloved old truck lacked. "Winnie took all the smaller party decorations in her car this morning.

She and Betty Lou will get there early to make sure the space is ready." "Won't Lillian see her car?"

"I sure hope not. Winnie is dropping off the decorations and leaving Betty Lou to get started while she drives around the corner to park her car. I told you, they're serious about the surprise," Annie said when Tom raised his eyebrows.

"So how do they propose I get in there unnoticed with a truck full of flowers?"

"Winnie assures me that by the time you arrive, Lillian will be in the dayroom at the back of the building in her book club meeting."

"So," Tom mused, "if Lillian decides to skip her book club?"

"Then it's all for nothing," Annie finished Tom's statement. "Pray that doesn't happen, Tom. This means a lot to Winnie and Betty Lou."

"Ryan's going to be sorry he missed this," Tom said as he started toward the pile of plants and decorations he was in charge of delivering.

"Maybe," Annie replied, heading back to the front of the shop, "but Winnie made arrangements with the kitchen to save him a big piece of cake with lots of frosting."

"Just like he likes it." Tom smiled as he backed out the door with his first armful of plants.

Like father, like son, Annie thought.

"Where do you want me to put this?" Tom called to Betty Lou as he entered the party room with Lillian's birthday present.

"Oh, me, That Annie sure outdid herself on this one!" Betty Lou exclaimed.

"Over here, Tom," Winnie called to him from the front table. We're going to put it behind the curtain here and show it to her just as we get ready to cut the cake."

"Betty Lou did a marvelous job on the cake too. She's going to be so surprised with that and all the flowers on the table."

"Not to mention us pulling off a surprise!" Betty Lou added happily. "First time in thirty years," she said, looking at her childhood friend. "That Lillian is so clever, who would've thought we could make this happen, Winnie?"

"Not me, that's for sure. We couldn't have done it without our friends though."

It wasn't long before the room was transformed into an indoor garden party with all the flowers and plants provided by Annie specifically for this occasion. Moments after the final place settings were set, Lillian walked in, expecting to pick up a box of teabags that Eva specially ordered through the kitchen. Her roommate had arranged the ruse the night before to ensure that Lillian would be present at the party held in her honor.

"I'd like to propose a toast to the birthday girl," Betty Lou said, raising her glass to Lillian. "We have been friends for longer than I can even remember," she began. "Winnie and I realized that neither of us can remember a time when we weren't friends. That may be just our memories slipping," she said to the small group gathered for the party, "but we agreed that it wouldn't matter even if we could." She smiled and winked at her friend as they toasted Lillian.

"Hear, hear!" Winnie said, raising her glass to Lillian. "And I'd like to propose a toast too," she said, standing up and raising her glass. "To Annie and Tom Walsh, you are so special to us. We appreciate you and all you do for us— including helping us pull off Lillian's first surprise party in thirty years! We couldn't have done this without you."

"Nor would we have wanted to," Betty Lou said, raising her glass. "The cake is absolutely beautiful, Betty Lou," Lillian told her friend as they sat down to eat. "Thank you so much."

"Don't forget, we have to save a piece for Ryan," Winnie said to the servers. "He likes lots of frosting."

As they were enjoying the birthday cake, Lillian made her way around the tables to thank her friends for coming. They lingered over their cake and coffee, making no effort to leave. When Lillian returned to her seat, Winnie called for everyone's attention.

"We have a special gift for you, Lillian," Winnie began. "It's from all of us to you." She nodded at Tom, who now stood beside the curtain covering the wall behind the head table.

As Tom pulled the curtain aside, Lillian turned to see what he was doing. "It's spectacular," she said softly, tears in her eyes. She looked knowingly at Annie and turned to hug her.

"I don't know what to say," she said, looking at her two closest friends. "You have truly made this birthday special. Thank you."

As she hugged Winnie and Betty Lou, they began to regale her with tales of the lengths they had gone to in keeping this party a secret from her. The gift of the flower garden had turned out beautifully. As promised, Annie hired one of the local artisans to personalize the container by painting the fencing and adding personal touches that included a watering can, a flower basket, and a birdhouse that looked just like Lillian's old home. "I'll take that upstairs for you when you're ready," Tom told her as he hugged her. Annie was making her rounds to the tables, ensuring that everyone knew the flowers in the centerpieces were individual vases intended as party favors.

56

"He said to tell you he was sorry and then just left."

"I'm so disappointed," Mary told her husband as they finished the dinner dishes and sat down at Annie's kitchen table to talk. Annie, Tom, and Ryan had taken the old truck into town for ice cream, but Pete and Mary begged off so they could talk privately about Pete's meeting with Arvin.

"Me too," he said putting his big hand over hers. "I don't think I realized how much until just now. It seemed like such a win-win situation. We get to be close to Annie and her family, and I get to rebuild a house with Tom and Ryan."

"He didn't give you any hint as to why he won't sell?"

"Not a clue. When I first proposed buying the house, his only question was why. I thought he was shocked because he didn't see any value in the place. Maybe he realized that he didn't want to let it go, even after everything that's happened."

"Well, we aren't going to let this stop us from finding the perfect place. After all, we didn't know the place was even an option before we got here, so we're not actually out anything. Don't worry, honey. You'll find another fixer-upper that you boys can work on together while we stay at Eva's for a while longer."

"I knew I married a keeper," Pete said as he put his arms around his wife and held her close.

"Oh no, not you guys too!" Ryan exclaimed as he ran in through the back door, catching his grandparents kissing in the kitchen. He rolled his eyes and shook his head at the scene before him. "I'm going to my room," he announced loudly to his parents as they came in the door right behind him.

"What's wrong?" Annie asked her mother.

"Nothing dear, just enjoying a moment with your father," she said as she smiled in his direction.

"Are you sure? You sort of look like you just got bad news." Mary looked at Pete, who nodded slightly. "We were hoping to surprise you, but it didn't work out. We found what we thought was the perfect home for us, but the owner said he isn't interested in selling. "Oh, that is bad news. Did he say why?"

"No, he didn't give a reason. But it's his decision, and we respect that.

We'll just keep looking!" she said brightly.

"I'm sure you'll find the perfect place soon enough. In the meantime, I know Eva's happy to have you renting her home."

"Speaking of home," Mary said, glancing at Pete, "I think we're going to go and let you two relax after your busy day. You both did an amazing job on Lillian's party."

"It was fun," Annie said with a yawn, "but I am beaten. Thanks for cooking dinner for us. I love having you so close by," she said with a smile as she hugged her mother and father in turn.

57

"Oh my gosh! You're pregnant!"

"What? No, I'm just..." Annie objected quickly, her words trailing off as she thought about what Becca had just said.

"Pregnant," Becca said again, smiling broadly at her closest friend.

"Could it be?" Annie said aloud, trying to think back over the past few weeks when she had been feeling so tired. *And a little queasy when I first get up*, she thought.

"Oh my gosh!" Annie said as the realization hit her. She saw Becca smiling at her, nodding her head as it started to sink in. "Okay," Becca said decisively, "finish your lunch, and we'll stop by the drug store before we go back to the shop."

They'd decided to grab a quick lunch at the deli down the street when Becca had a last-minute cancellation.

"I'm done," Annie said quickly, wrapping the other half of her turkey sandwich in the wrapper and sliding it into her purse. "Let's go."

The two friends didn't speak until they'd returned to Blooms, heading directly into the restroom. Becca handed Annie the stick with an encouraging smile and waited for her to emerge with the completed test.

"Now what?" Annie asked.

"Now we wait," Becca answered calmly. Not because she wasn't excited but because she had been through this before and knew the routine. "How long?"

"Three minutes."

"How long has it been?"

"One minute, twenty seconds." "How much longer?"

"One minute." "Now?"

"Now."

"I can't look. You look first." "Are you sure?"

"What if it's positive?" Annie said nervously. "Or what if it's not?" "Look," Becca said, smiling and showing Annie the results window with two solid lines.

"That's a positive," Annie said, stunned at the result. "That's a positive," Becca confirmed, reaching out to hug her friend.

58

"Mmm," Tom said as he lifted the lid of the large pot simmering on the stovetop. "Beef stew. And home-made biscuits," he added as he noticed Ryan cutting out the dough on the kitchen countertop. "You know that's my favorite. What's the occasion?"

"No occasion," Annie replied with a knowing smile. "Just making my man happy. How was your day?"

"It just keeps getting better and better," Tom replied cheerfully. We got the new golf course job," he announced proudly, wrapping his arms around Annie's waist and kissing her as she turned her head to look at him. "Congratulations, honey. That's great news. Is that the one in Nashville where they're building separate areas that all link together?"

"It is. There will be a pool house, a clubhouse, and a small conference center with twenty guest rooms. And on top of that, they are already considering increasing the scope to include a dozen individual bungalows around the lake. There will be multiple levels and terraces that connect the main buildings as well as both indoor and outdoor pool areas. It's going to be something. I can't wait to get started!"

"Okay, Mom, these are ready," Ryan said as he checked on the first batch of biscuits."

Tom continued to fill her in on the details of the deal as he set the table. Ryan filled the water glasses as Annie dished up the stew. Within minutes, they were sitting down to a nice dinner. *A dinner that would be followed by more good news*, Annie thought as she took her seat at the table. This was indeed a good day for them all.

As they sat at the kitchen table eating and talking, Annie felt a memory in the making. Their lives were about to change significantly.

She refocused on the conversation when she realized Tom was still talking to her.

"…Traveling a lot more. I know that's not ideal," Tom continued, "but this is a great opportunity. If we can break into the resort market successfully with this job, it opens up a whole new…"

Did he just say traveling a lot more?

Annie was no longer sure the timing of her news was the best idea. She'd have to think about it some more before telling Tom. She had already decided that she would let him tell Ryan when and how he thought it best.

Maybe I'll just give it a few days, she thought. *Let him enjoy his good news for tonight. After all, my news was not going away. I'll just have to remember to tell Becca that he doesn't know yet.*

"Annie?" Tom asked, taking her hand. "Are you okay? You seem a million miles away," he said as he watched her closely.

"Hmm? Oh no, I'm fine." She recovered quickly from her reverie, determined not to spoil Tom's evening. "I was just thinking about how that would work with you traveling so much."

"You don't have to worry about that, Annie," Tom said reassuringly. "The job won't start for a few weeks due to the long holiday weekend. When it does, I will do most of the initial work from here and only travel to Nashville or DC to meet with the developers and investors as needed. I've already contacted my team in LA, and they are ready to step in and do the heavy lifting once the designs are complete. I just meant that I would be taking a few trips throughout the project to do presentations and check on progress. None of that will happen until after the New Year though."

"Oh, good," Annie said, visibly relieved. "I just wasn't sure how I was going to handle it all if you were gone."

"Handle all what, Annie?" Tom asked his wife, noticing that she seemed preoccupied.

"I can help," Ryan spoke up quickly. "Dad's taught me how to do a lot around here, and I'm almost as strong as he is. Right, Dad?" Ryan asked his father excitedly.

Tom didn't answer him right away. He was focused on Annie, who looked like she was about to cry.

"Uh, that's right, honey, Ryan is growing up fast. In fact," he said, turning to Ryan, "can you do me a favor and check to see if I left the generator on in the barn? I had it running earlier, and I don't want to forget it."

"Sure thing," Ryan said as he quickly rose, grabbing his coat as he headed out the back door.

Tom kept his eyes on Annie as he reached over and turned her chair around to face him. "Okay, tell me what's going on. You look like you're about to cry. Is it the new job? Did something happen at the shop? Talk to me, Annie."

"No," she said, "it's just…"

Tom waited for her to find her words, hoping Ryan didn't return before he found out why his wife was happy one moment and ready to cry the next.

"I saw Becca today," she began, "and there is a half-sandwich in my bag. Do you want it?" she asked her husband.

"No, I'm good," he said with a small grin, noting that Annie was trying to tell him something, but her mind was racing.

"Oh right, dinner," she said with a glance at the table. "So you saw Becca today?"

"Yes, and there were two lines, Tom. Two pink lines!" she said as she burst into tears and hugged him tightly. Suddenly realizing that he hadn't said anything, she stepped back and looked at his confused expression. "We're going to have a baby, Tom. I'm pregnant." She smiled through her tears.

"Whoo-hoo!" Ryan yelled as he let the door slam behind him. "I'm going to have a baby brother!"

"Or sister," Tom said softly, looking into Annie's eyes as he cupped her face and kissed her. "A baby," Tom said happily. "Our baby."

"Our baby," Annie replied, opening her arms to include Ryan in their little circle.

59

"I'm telling you, she's showing all the signs," Winnie insisted as she and Betty Lou headed to Magnolia Lane to pick up Lillian for Thanksgiving dinner at Tom and Annie's house.

"I sure hope you're right," Betty Lou said, smiling.

"I am. And as soon as she figures it out, I'm sure she and Tom will tell us all."

"Has she been to see Lillian lately? I know she's been busy with the holiday arrangements for the store. I also heard that she has two weddings between now and Christmas. I don't know how she keeps up with it all now that she has a family."

"Things are different these days, Betty Lou. From what I've seen, Tom is a big help around the house. And Ryan does his share as well. I can only imagine how things will change with a baby in the house, but they're young, and they'll figure it out. It's so exciting, don't you think?" Winnie asked, her blue eyes dancing.

"It will be nice to have a baby in the family," Betty Lou agreed.

"Mom, remember when you offered to help at the shop?" Annie asked her mother as they peeled their way through the massive pile of potatoes for dinner that afternoon.

"Of course, whatever you need," Mary replied.

"I could use your help at the shop for the next several months. The holidays are a busy time for us, and with the baby coming, I am going to need all the help I can get."

"Baby?" Pete asked as he looked incredulously at Tom. "Baby," Tom confirmed with a nod and a huge grin.

"Annie is in the kitchen telling Mary as we speak."

Pete stood up to shake Tom's hand and hug his proud son-in-law. "Congratulations, Tom. That is wonderful news!" As they went up the basement stairs into the kitchen with the extra chairs for dinner, Tom saw Annie and her mother hugging and crying.

"Oh, Pete," Mary said through her tears, "we're going to be grandparents again!" She smiled and reached out to hug her husband.

"So I take it this is good news then?" Tom asked jokingly. "It's the best news!" Mary replied to Tom as she turned to hug him. "I'm so happy for you two."

"And us!" Pete added. "I'm happy for us too!"

"When are you due?" Mary asked suddenly as she turned to look at Annie.

"June nineteenth," Annie replied with a smile as Tom walked over and put his arm around her.

"Does Ryan know?" Pete asked.

"He does," Tom answered, "and he couldn't be happier. Last night when he first found out, he was hoping for a baby brother. Then this morning, he told us that he'd be just as happy with a baby sister."

60

"We'd like to thank you all for sharing Thanksgiving dinner with us this year," Tom said as he stood at the head of the table behind a very large turkey, carving tools in hand.

"Annie and I would like to continue my family's tradition of giving thanks by asking everyone to tell us one thing they are thankful for. As we go around the table, please take a moment to reflect on what it is that makes you happy and fulfilled in your life." Tom looked to his mother seated to his left and nodded at her to start.

As they went around the table, Tom was heartened to hear so many of his friends and family express thankfulness to God for the many blessings in their lives. The grandparents were thankful for family and continued good health, while the children were thankful for the food and fun they were having with each other. The Jameson's were thankful for such wonderful friends and healthy children, and Annie smiled lovingly at Tom as he went last, sharing their happy news.

"I am thankful for so many blessings," Tom began, "but for the sake of eating our meal while it's still warm, and because I'm about to burst with the news, I've chosen just one. I'm so thankful to my beautiful wife for giving me another child to love."

As the cheers went up around the table, Winnie looked knowingly at Betty Lou. "Whoo-hoo!" she exclaimed loudly. "That's the best news I've heard since your engagement!"

"How far along are you?" Lillian asked.

"My due date is June nineteenth," Annie told her. "We know it's still early, but we just couldn't wait to tell you. The doctor said it's pretty safe after the first trimester, and although we aren't there yet, Tom and I decided that our friends are family to us, and we wanted all our family to know."

61

"I'm glad you're here," Annie said to Susannah. "We missed you at Thanksgiving." She and Susannah were at the toy store with Ryan, encouraging him to get an early start on his Christmas list. With so many grandparents looking for ideas, they were happy to just let him add anything he wanted.

"I can't believe I missed the big announcement!" Susannah said with disappointment as they followed Ryan into the toy truck aisle.

"I can't believe Arvin came for dinner," Annie said with a laugh.

"You win!" Susannah said cheerfully, indicating that Annie's disbelief was indeed greater than her own.

"Did he know that Mom and Dad weren't coming?" she asked, assuming that was why the man had agreed to attend.

"I'm not sure," Annie told her. "He may have asked Ryan, but he never said a word to me or Tom."

"Do you think he'll come to the party on Christmas Eve?" Susannah asked, knowing her parents were planning to be there through the holidays. "Honestly, I think he will," Annie replied. "He has become much more social with Tom and me, and with my parents since he found out Ryan was Maggie's son. He spends a lot of time with Ryan, teaching him all sorts of things. I think he is thrilled to have someone to carry on his legacy, if not his name," Annie concluded.

"How is your mom doing with all of this?" Annie asked, concerned that Charlotte was coming back to Magnolia Creek again for the first time since seeing Arvin at the wedding reception.

"I'm not positive," Susannah told Annie, "but she seems happier. Maybe not happier, I guess, but relieved."

"It must have been a burden all those years," Annie mused. "At first looking over her shoulder for Arvin to come after her and then at some point realizing that he wasn't coming. I can't begin to imagine the anxiety it caused her when you found Tom living in Magnolia Creek!" Annie added.

"And then, just to make it more complex," Susannah expounded, "he becomes engaged to the woman living right next door to her secret ex-husband!"

"Right?!" was all Annie could think to say as she and Susannah laughed at the absurdity of the situation.

"I have to be honest with you," Susannah told Annie. "I never would have guessed my mother had such an intriguing life."

"You are not alone," Annie said, smiling at Susannah.

62

"Annie?" Becca called out as she stepped through the back door and into the kitchen. "Tom said I should come in," she explained. "Annie?"

"Down here," she heard faintly from the direction of the basement stairs.

"Can I help?" Becca asked as she made her way down the stairs to where Annie was sorting through a box of what looked like Christmas decorations.

"You're just in time," Annie said, relieved to have the help. "I thought I remembered Grandma Abby having a string of sleigh bells in her decorations, but Tom said he didn't see them. I wanted to find them for the hayride with the kids."

"Here, let me get that," Becca said quickly as Annie reached for a large box. "You need to remember not to do too much reaching or lifting, at least for a little while longer."

"Thanks," Annie said with a hint of annoyance. "I'm sorry, Becca," she recovered quickly, "I don't know what's gotten into me. I know I need to remember that it's still early in my pregnancy, but I feel so helpless when anyone else is around. It's not like I'm on bed rest or anything. I'm completely fine."

"Well, I'd wager what's gotten into you is hormones," Becca said, smiling as she put the box on the floor in front of Annie. "Frankly, I say go with it. Let Tom and Ryan and anyone else around here help you."

"Easier said than done," Annie grumbled.

"Listen, we all know you are a very capable woman," Becca assured her friend. "We just care about you, and we want to help in some small way. It lets us feel closer to you."

"I never thought of it that way," Annie said, begin to cry. "Everyone is being so nice, and I'm being such a…"

"…Hormonal maniac?" her friend interjected.

"Okay sure," Annie said, wiping her tears, "let's go with that."

63

"Any luck?" Scott called down the stairs.

"You'll have to look in the barn," Annie replied. "Tell Tom there isn't anything even resembling sleigh bells down here."

"Gotcha," Scott replied as he turned and headed back outside.

"No luck?" Tom asked his friend when he saw that he returned from the house empty-handed.

"Nope, she said we should look for them out here," Scott explained. "I thought I'd kept everything together from last year, but those aren't in the corner with the other stuff. Hey, Ryan," Tom called, "have you seen the sleigh bells we used for the hayride last year?"

"I took them to the clubhouse," he said as he stuck his head over the edge of the old hayloft. He was checking their stock of hay bales and rolling them over the edge, one by one, onto the bed of the wagon below.

"Why would you need sleigh bells at the clubhouse?" he asked his son, slightly annoyed with himself that he hadn't thought to ask Ryan first. "Never mind, it doesn't matter. Can you please be sure to get them and bring them back before dark? I want to have the wagon all ready to go in the morning."

"Sure thing, Dad," Ryan replied cheerfully as he rolled another bale over the side of the loft.

"Anything I can do to help?" Pete asked as he came in through the side door. They'd decided to keep the front barn doors closed to keep at least some of the cold out while they were working in there.

"Sure," Tom said to his father-in-law "You have your pick—you can either help me arrange the hay bales on the wagon or Scott can help me and you can see what you can do to untangle those Christmas lights."

"Hay bales it is!" Pete said quickly. "Sorry, Scott." He smiled at the young man standing dejectedly over the box of lights. "I've done my time."

64

"Let's let the boys deal with this mess while you and I take another look at what still needs to be done for the party tomorrow."

As they climbed the stairs into the kitchen, they were surprised to find Annie's mom sitting at the kitchen table, drinking a cup of coffee.

"She does that," Annie said with a grin at her friend. "I can't tell you how many times I've walked into my kitchen and found my mom sitting there drinking her coffee."

"It's the sixth sense, dear. Wait and see, both of you. When your kids are grown and out of the house, you too will develop a sense of when you're needed," she explained sagely.

"Maybe," Annie granted, "but it doesn't hurt that Dad called this morning to say he was coming by early to help Tom with the tractor."

"You're right," Mary conceded with a sly smile. "That doesn't hurt at all." "Sixth sense or not Mary, we're glad you're here," Becca told her as she took a seat at the table.

"Guestlist," Becca said as she began reading off the checklist they'd prepared for the Christmas Eve party.

"Check," Annie replied.

"Are the Davidsons coming?" Mary asked her daughter. "Yes," Annie assured her. "They will be arriving in town tonight and staying with Betty Lou. Susannah is coming with them, but she's staying with

Rachel and Paul. She got quite close to Eva's granddaughter and her family while she was living here last year."

"And Arvin? Have you heard from him?" Mary continued. "He will be here as well," she said. "It should make for an interesting evening."

"Did Kate hear back from Elizabeth?" Annie asked her mother, referring to Tom's younger sister.

"Yes, she went home first and is flying in with them tonight. They are all staying at our house," Mary explained to Becca.

"Nice," Becca said. "It sounds like everyone is accounted for."

"What about food?" Becca asked, continuing down the checklist she held in her hand.

They worked the rest of the day at it, but by dinnertime, the three women were done, and all the food that could be prepped the day before was ready.

65

Annie sat by the fire with her feet propped up on a stool. She had been gently kicked out of her kitchen and told to get off her feet by practically every mother in attendance, including her own.

What a crazy, beautiful party, Annie thought. Unlike most people she knew who reflected on their lives as the New Year approached, Annie had always been one to take stock at Christmas. Perhaps it was the feeling of family closeness that the holidays evoked, or maybe it was just happy memories of everyone being together. Whatever the reason, it was as good a time as any to reflect on her life.

"Penny for your thoughts," Lillian said as she sat down next to Annie, laying her hand gently on Annie's arm.

"You don't have to pay for my thoughts," Annie said lovingly to the older woman. "You're as much a part of my wonderful life here as Tom and Ryan."

"I don't know about that," Lillian replied modestly.

"I do," Annie told her, taking her hand as she did so. "Grandma Abby knew exactly what she was doing, didn't she?" Annie asked her grandmother's closest friend.

"It sure seems like it to me," Lillian responded with a wistful smile. "You miss her a lot, don't you?" Annie asked her.

"I do," Lillian replied honestly, "but I'm thankful every day that I'm not missing a moment of this," she said, squeezing Annie's hand.

66

"I could use your advice," Arvin said softly to the two other men in the room. He had been waiting patiently since before dinner to get an opportunity to speak with Harrison and Frederick alone. He was in desperate need of advice, and he was sure these were the men to ask.

"Sure, Arvin. What do you need?" Frederick offered.

"I need some legal advice that has to do with providing for Ryan," Arvin explained in hushed tones, "and I don't know where to start."

"How about we go into Tom's study so we can talk privately?" Harrison suggested, picking up on the fact that Arvin had waited until they were alone to broach the subject.

As the three men entered Tom's study and Harrison closed the door, Arvin began.

"Pete Reed recently approached me about selling him a property that I own. He wants to remodel the house, rebuild the barn, and make it a nice place for him and Mary to live in," he explained.

"Okay," Harrison said, understanding that the other man needed more time to get to the point. "Go on."

"The thing is," Arvin said delicately, "it's where Charlene and I lived when we were married. Sorry," he said to Frederick, "I mean Charlotte," referring to his ex-wife's preferred name.

"It's okay, Arvin. She was Charlene when you knew her. Call her whatever you're comfortable with," he said sincerely, "but just know that when talking to her, she prefers Charlotte," he said with a conspiratorial smile.

"Thanks," Arvin said to Frederick, "but the problem isn't with her."

"Then how can we help you?" Harrison asked.

"I plan to leave all my possessions, including that property, to Ryan, who is my only heir," Arvin explained to the gentlemen seated in the chairs opposite his.

"I see," Frederick spoke first. "You don't have an issue with them fixing up the place and living there. You just want to make sure it stays in the family. Your family," Frederick clarified.

"Exactly. When Pete first asked me," Arvin explained, "I told him it wasn't for sale. Ryan's young," he explained. "Since he doesn't need it now, it seems like it would be a good place for them to be, you know, close to the family and the new baby."

"So, if I understand you correctly," Harrison began, "you'd like to legally transfer ownership to them until they no longer want or need the property at which time it will legally revert to Ryan, superseding all claims, regardless of their wills.

"If that means they fix it up and live there and then give it back to Ryan, then yes," Arvin replied.

"Do you want them to pay you for the property now?" Frederick asked. "Or are you proposing their investment in the improvements would suffice?"

"I haven't thought about that part," Arvin said honestly, "I just want to know if it can be done so Ryan can have the home where his mother was born."

"Yes," both men assured him, "it can be done."

"Then what do I do next?" Arvin asked. "Do I tell them what I want to do or hire a lawyer first?"

"I think you might want to talk with a local lawyer and have him help you figure out exactly what you want to do as far as selling or leasing long-term," Harrison advised the other man. "Then you should talk with Pete and Mary and see if they are interested in proceeding with those restrictions," he added. "You might find that they will be more than agreeable to that since the land will revert to Ryan."

"Thank you," Arvin said earnestly, shaking each man's hand in turn.

67

"Charlotte," Kate said, "you look radiant this evening." She'd been waiting for some time now for an opportunity to speak to Charlotte alone, but she tended to stick very close to Frederick. When Frederick went into the study with Harrison and Arvin, she found her chance.

"Thank you, Kate," Charlotte replied, pleased at the compliment. "It was a wonderful dinner," she added pleasantly. "So nice to have everyone together."

"It is," Kate agreed. "We missed you at Thanksgiving. Susannah tells me you were on an extended cruise. How did you find that much time at sea?" she inquired, keeping the conversation light.

"Quite enjoyable. We were fortunate to have good weather, and the Mediterranean is just beautiful at this time of year."

"I think Ryan's grown a foot since the wedding," Kate remarked of the grandson the two women shared.

"So much like his mother," Charlotte said longingly. "I miss her so much, especially at the holidays."

"I shudder to think about what you must go through, losing your child," Kate said sympathetically. "I can't imagine."

"And you don't want to," Charlotte confessed to Tom's mother. "I wish I'd known her," Kate said sincerely to Maggie's mother.

"In a way, you do. Ryan is so much like her," she admitted. "Kind, thoughtful, intelligent. She and Tom were very much alike. I often wondered how they ended up together with so many similarities."

"Thank you for that," Kate said, touching the other woman's arm, "for searching out Tom and allowing us to be a part of Ryan's life."

Charlotte started to say something, then thought better of it. She just looked down at her hands resting in her lap. Kate saw the tear fall just before spoke again.

"I did not want to upset you, Charlotte. I truly didn't," Kate said honestly. "I just wanted to tell you how much I admire you."

"For what?" Charlotte asked, stunned by Kate's words. "I was a coward," she admitted, "I didn't want to find Tom. I wanted to keep Ryan to myself, just like I did with Maggie," she said sadly.

"But you didn't, Charlotte. What happened in the past is over. Whatever your reasoning was at the time, when it came right down to it, you did the right thing. You gave that boy the chance to know his father," Kate continued earnestly.

When the other woman didn't respond, Kate continued. "Charlotte, you came back to Magnolia Creek after all these years and faced Maggie's father. You did that. That took an incredible amount of courage," Kate said slowly and emphatically, "and that is admirable."

Kate shifted her seat to sit directly beside the other woman and put her arm around her. Kate had felt the need to encourage Charlotte since the first time they met. She could not put herself in the other woman's shoes without feeling her sadness and desperation. Whatever her faults and choices, Charlotte Davidson deserved to have someone in her corner.

68

"It's so peaceful here," Pete said to Mary as they sat huddled together on the wooden bench in the orchard. They'd visited this site several times since her mother passed, remembering how Abby would come here to feel close to her Ben after he passed. Tonight seemed like a special time for Mary to come

here with Pete to reflect on her parents and their daughter and her family.

"Peaceful and cold," Mary said, shivering slightly.

Pete lifted her off the cold bench, sat her on his lap, and wrapped his arms around her to keep her warm. "Better?" he asked.

"Much," she replied as she rested her head on his chest. "Glad to be home?" Pete continued as he nuzzled the top of her head.

"There's honestly no place I'd rather be at this very moment," she said contentedly.

"It's even better than last year," Tom said to Annie as they stole a moment alone on the front porch. The Christmas lights were shining bright, the driveway was full of cars, and Brenda Lee's Christmas album was playing in the background.

"I think the same can be said of your scavenger hunt," Annie told him. "The kids couldn't wait to finish dinner so they could head back out to the barn to embellish your stories and play with their treasures."

"I have to admit, I love it as much as they do," he told his wife. "More than they do," she said to him with certainty. "Oh, and I want my turkey baster back."

"About that," he said as he pulled her closer to him, "I think you're going to need to ask Santa for a new one."

www.ingramcontent.com/pod-product-compliance
Lightning Source LLC
Chambersburg PA
CBHW021443070526
44577CB00002B/260